DAILY VICTORY

"HE GIVES US THE VICTORY THROUGH OUR LORD JESUS CHRIST" I CORINTHIANS 15:57

Character

Building

Devotions

for Young

People

by Chuck Smith

Cover Design: Jean Holmgren
Printing: Chauncey Johnson Printing and Advertising
           Memphis, Tennessee

Author's Note: The stories within these devotional thoughts come
from everywhere. It would be impossible to give credit to all of those
who have inspired me over the years. My gratitude to those who
have.

To order additional copies:

VP

Victory Publications
P.O. Box 11056
Memphis, TN 38111-0056

Phone: (901)759-5915
www.dailyvictory.net
e-mail: smith@dailyvictory.net

ACKNOWLEDGMENTS

I would like to express my sincere appreciation to everyone who encouraged and supported me along the way.

Special thanks to my wife, Sonya, and our three sons for their help in deciding those devotions that "made the cut" and were included in the book.

Special thanks to Dr. Len Sumner, Larry Rea, and Evelyn Foote for their help in editing the book.

Special thanks to Steve Peckham at Chauncey Johnson Printing and Advertising.

I thank my God every time I remember you.   Philippians 1:3

DEDICATION

TO DENNIS SMITH

My brother

My friend

My partner in ministry

Thanks for your encouragement and support in this project.

INTRODUCTION

God, who has called you into fellowship with his Son Jesus Christ our Lord. I Corinthians 1:9

We were created to know God. A vital part of any relationship is TIME. The aim of this book is to provide young people with a Devotion-A-Day so that they may know God more intimately, enjoy His fellowship, and experience *Daily Victory* as they face the challenges of living in the real world.

"Sweet Victory"

He gives us the victory through our Lord Jesus Christ.

I Corinthians 15:57

The North Carolina State basketball team finished the regular season with just 17 wins and 10 losses. They were not ranked, not respected, and it seemed that they had little chance of even qualifying for the NCAA tournament. But the unexpected happened when the team won its conference championship and was given the league's automatic bid.

Entering the NCAA tournament, Coach Jim Valvano's motto for the team was "survive and advance." The North Carolina State Wolfpack then fought their way past four teams on their way to the championship game against the top-ranked and heavily favored Houston Cougars with Akeem Olajuwon.

With just a few seconds remaining and the score tied at 52-52, N.C. State guard Derek Wittenburg launched a 30-foot desperation shot. The ball fell short. But teamate Lorenzo Charles was in position to dunk the missed shot for the win and the NCAA championship. The N.C. State Wolfpack became the first team to win the NCAA with 10 or more losses in the regular season. Some have called the victory the "greatest Cinderella story" in basketball history.

While many consider N.C. State's win over Houston one of college basketball's greatest victories, surely the greatest victory of all time was won by the Lord Jesus Christ. Through his death, burial and resurrection Jesus has won an awesome victory over sin and death. That victory becomes our victory when we place our faith in Jesus and become part of His team. Not only do we receive forgiveness from sin and eternal life but He becomes our hope and help in times of trouble.

The Influence of One Life

Remember this: Whoever sows sparingly will also reap sparingly, and whoever sows generously will also reap generously. Each man should give what he has decided in his heart to give, not reluctantly or under compulsion, for God loves a cheerful giver.

II Corinthians 9:6-7

Osceola McCarty dropped out of school in the sixth grade to support her family and spent much of the rest of her life working. In fact, she never married and never had children. What she did do was take in the dirty clothes of others and then washed and ironed them. Living in rural Mississippi, Osceola didn't earn a lot of money for her work. The truth is, she never earned more than $9,000 a year. But most of what she did earn, she saved. Osceola started at age eight saving a few cents a week.

When she finally retired after working 75 years, she was shocked to discover that her bank balance had grown to more than $150,000. Miss Osceola McCarty then became a national celebrity when she donated the entire amount to help black students in Mississippi go to college. She simply stated, "I wanted to share my wealth with the children."

In II Corinthians 9:6-7 Paul compares giving to a farmer planting seed. If he plants sparingly he can expect only a meager harvest. But the opposite is also true; if he plants generously he can expect a bountiful return in due time. When I truly give of my resources, the influence of my life is multiplied. My resources then not only benefit me, but also others, and the Kingdom of God.

Strength In Weakness

My grace is sufficient for you, for my power is made perfect in weakness.   II Corinthians 12:9

One of the most memorable scenes in Olympic history unfolded on the evening of August 3, 1992. The stadium of spectators watched as eight men lined up for the start of the 400 meter race. Among them was Derek Redmond of Great Britain, considered to be one of the favorites to win a medal. Just four years earlier at the Olympics in Korea, he also had a chance at a medal but withdrew just prior to the race because of a pulled tendon. Since that time Redmond's career had been plagued by injuries.

When the starting gun sounded, Redmond got off to a strong start. He looked good and moved quickly around the track. But as he neared the halfway point, there was a strange pop. Derek Redmond had torn a hamstring muscle in his right leg. Grimacing in pain, he stood motionless on the track as the other runners finished the race.

Suddenly a man came running from the stands, rushed past the medics carrying a stretcher and caught up to the injured runner. It was Jim Redmond, Derek's father. The world watched the father and son's emotional embrace. Then, arm-in-arm, Jim Redmond helped his son around the track and to the finish line. Together they gained Olympic glory even in defeat.

The Bible clearly teaches us in Ephesian 2:8 that God's grace is able to save us from our sin. Surely His grace is also able to assist us as we live the Christian life. God is more than able to encourage and help us as we experience trials and troubles. In our weakness, He is strong. Just as Jim Redmond helped his son to the finish line, our difficulties are simply opportunities for God to reveal His grace, strengthen us to continue living the Christian life, and "finish the race."

Living Up To Your Name

*Let your light shine before men, that they may see your good deeds
and praise your Father in heaven.*   Matthew 5:16

Alexander the Great was king of Macedonia and one of the
greatest military leaders in all history. He was fearless, strong, and
full of ambition. At the height of his power, Alexander's kingdom
included most of the civilized world. Once, while on a military
campaign, he discovered one of his soldiers asleep on guard duty.
As Alexander approached, the soldier awoke and began to tremble
with fear. The penalty for such an offense was oftentimes death.
Sometimes the sleeping soldier would even be doused with kerosene
and set afire while he was still sleeping.

Alexander asked the soldier, "Do you know the penalty for
sleeping on guard duty?" With trembling voice the soldier
answered, "Yes, sir." Alexander the Great then asked the soldier's
name. The soldier responded, "Alexander, sir." Alexander the
Great forcefully asked the soldier the same question a second time.
The soldier nervously replied, "My name is Alexander, sir."
Staring the young soldier in the eye, Alexander the Great stated,
"Soldier, either change your name or change your conduct."

As believers in the Lord Jesus Christ, we must never forget
that we bear His name as "Christians." When others see our love
and good works, we bring honor and praise to the name of Christ.
But when we sin and the world sees words and actions that are not
Christ-like, we bring dishonor and shame to His name. Remember
the old hymn:

Let others see Jesus in you.
Let others see Jesus in you.
Keep telling the story,
be faithful and true.
Let others see Jesus in you.

4

Prayer Power

Do not be anxious about anything, but in everything, by prayer and petition, with thanksgiving, present your requests to God.

Philippians 4:6

David Jacobsen, head of the largest hospital in West Beirut, was a man of power and position. But one day in 1985 everything changed for the American. Jacobsen was taken hostage by three men wearing hoods and carrying machine guns. After being bound and gagged, he was taken to the hideout of the terrorists and chained to a wall. He was hated and treated terribly. Once a day Jacobsen and the other hostages were fed a mush of water, rice, and lentils that was hardly fit to eat.

Discouraged and fearful of torture and death at the hands of the terrorists, the prisoners often gathered together, held hands, and prayed to God. While some men are broken by such difficulties, David Jacobsen's faith was strengthened, and God gave him a sense of peace and comfort. He spent 17 months as a hostage in Beirut. The final three months were spent in a six foot-by-six foot cell all alone. But in November 1986 David Jacobsen was released and given back his freedom.

Prayer is simply a way of communicating with God. As we voice our needs and concerns to Him, our prayers have the power to change not only our circumstances but also to change us. Our prayers are an act of faith and dependence upon a God who loves us more than we can imagine. He is our Heavenly Father. And just as any good father provides for the needs of his children, our God takes care of His own.

Who We Really Are

For you created my inmost being; you knit me together in my mother's womb. I praise you because I am fearfully and wonderfully made; your works are wonderful, I know that full well.

Psalm 139:13-14

An old Indian story tells of a young brave who found an eagle's egg. He placed the egg into the nest of a prairie chicken. Soon afterwards all of the eggs hatched, and the eaglet grew up with the chicks. Never knowing he was an eagle, he did what prairie chickens do. All of his life he spent his days clucking and scratching around in the dirt with the other chickens looking for seeds or insects. From time to time he would flap his wings furiously and fly a few feet just like he saw the others do.

One day when he was very old he saw a bird soaring high above in the crystal blue sky. He marveled at the beautiful bird that flew so effortlessly in the heavens. "What is it?" he asked. The chicken next to him replied, "Why that's an eagle, the most glorious and graceful of all birds. But don't give it a second thought; you'll never be like him." Thoughtfully he took one last look toward the skies and then went back to scratching in the dirt. And so he lived out the rest of his days with those prairie chickens thinking he was one of them. He died never knowing he was an eagle.

Oftentimes you and I are like the eagle who spent his life scratching around in the dirt with prairie chickens. We either don't know - or perhaps have just forgotten - who we really are. Each of our lives have great value because we were lovingly and carefully created by the God of the universe. An accurate understanding of who we are will significantly impact the way we live day-by-day.

"Looks Can Fool You"

But the LORD said to Samuel, "Do not consider his appearance or his height, for I have rejected him. The LORD does not look at the things man looks at. Man looks at the outward appearance, but the LORD looks at the heart."   I Samuel 16:7

At a height of only 5-7 and weighing barely more than 100 pounds, 17-year-old Audie Murphy walked into the Marine recruiting office. Just six months after the bombing of Pearl Harbor had brought the United States into World War II, Murphy was determined to become a soldier. But when the Marine sergeant looked over the baby-faced farmboy, he was turned down. When he was also rejected by the paratroopers, Murphy ate as much as possible to gain weight and he was finally accepted by the Army. During his early days of training, he fainted on the drill field and the other soldiers began calling him "baby."

When he was assigned to cooks' and bakers' school, he refused to go. Later when an officer took pity on the baby-faced recruit and assigned him to a desk job, Murphy again refused. Finally he completed his infantry training and was assigned to the 3rd Infantry Division in North Africa.

During a fierce battle in Italy, he shot two enemy officers. Because of his marksmanship and skills as a soldier, he was quickly promoted to corporal and then to sergeant. He earned a Bronze Star when he destroyed an enemy tank and led his men to safety amidst heavy machine-gun attack. In 1944, Murphy almost single-handedly captured an enemy-held hill and was awarded the nation's second highest decoration for bravery, a Distinguished Service Cross. His acts of bravery did not end there. When the war ended Lieutenant Audie Murphy had received 23 decorations for his skill and bravery and became the most decorated soldier in the history of the United States.

We often make judgments about other people based on their

outward appearance. But as you may have already heard, "looks can fool you." Our judgments of other people are often terribly wrong. God makes it clear in His Word that He is not concerned about our height, weight, physical strength, or beauty. God's focus is on the thing that really matters. He looks at the inward appearance - our character.

Training For Perfection

Train yourself to be godly. For physical training is of some value, but godliness has value for all things, holding promise for both the present life and the life to come. I Timothy 4:7-8

Early in the 1989 college basketball season, Michigan played Wisconsin. It was a tight game late in the fourth quarter when Rumeal Robinson of Michigan stepped to the free throw line for two shots. He had an opportunity to regain the lead for Michigan but missed both shots. Wisconsin went on to win the game. Rumeal felt that his missed free throws cost Michigan the game, and he felt awful. For the remainder of the season he shot 100 extra free throws at the end of each practice. While his teammates showered off and relaxed in their dorms, Rumeal tirelessly worked to perfect his shooting.

Michigan made it all the way to the national championship game that same season. With three seconds left in overtime, Rumeal Robinson again stepped to the free throw line to shoot two free throws. He made both shots and Michigan won the championship.

Training is a must if you want to be a success in sports. There is no substitute for hard work. There are no shortcuts. The secret of success is practice, practice, practice.

The Bible clearly tells believers to "train yourself to be godly." Godly living means living like the Lord Jesus Christ in our attitudes, actions, and words. This kind of life comes through training. There are no shortcuts. We must live by faith, study God's Word, pray, attend Church regularly, and obey His commandments. Remember, a godly life is a life that is pleasing to God, a life that God blesses.

The Untamed Tongue

All kinds of animals, birds, reptiles and creatures of the sea are being tamed and have been tamed by man, but no man can tame the tongue. It is a restless evil, full of deadly poison. James 4:7-8

An adult lion can be up to 9 feet long and weigh up to 500 pounds. Its top speed is 10 miles per hour faster than the world's fastest human, and he can leap nearly 30 feet. The lion can eat up to 75 pounds of meat in one meal and can single-handedly drag a 600 pound water buffalo. Lions are so fierce they can disable or kill with a single swipe of the paw, and they have even been known to attack baby elephants. No wonder he is called the king of the jungle.

Yet, for hundreds of years men have mastered, tamed, and controlled this king of the jungle. Ancient Egyptian history tells us that Pharaoh Ramses II tamed a lion and took it into battle as a mascot. Roman history records the story of a ruler who even rode in a chariot pulled by a team of lions. The *Guinness Book of World Records* tells of the incredible feats of lion tamer Captain Alfred Schneider, who in 1925 climbed into a cage of 40 lions without the protection of a whip, stick, or gun.

The Bible says the tongue cannot be tamed. In fact, James goes on to say in 3:9-10, "With the tongue we praise our Lord and Father, and with it we curse men, who have been made in God's likeness. Out of the same mouth come praise and cursing. My brothers, this should not be." Our tongues have the power to praise God and encourage others. But our tongues also have the power to hurt when we use them to criticize, tease, or gossip. The tongue is tough to tame. But through God's help and the obedience to His commands we can begin to master our tongue and use it for good and not evil.

Getting Tripped Up

Let us throw off everything that hinders and the sin that so easily entangles, and let us run with perseverance the race marked out for us.   Hebrews 12:1

One of the greatest moments in Olympic history took place at the 1964 Games in Tokyo, Japan. Competing in the 10,000 meter run was an American Indian by the name of Billy Mills. Track and field experts didn't expect much from Billy. The unanimous favorite was world record holder Ron Clarke of Australia. Other favorites included Pyotr Bolotnikov, who won the event at the previous Olympics, and Murray Halberg, who won the 5,000 meter race days earlier.

Billy's strategy was to try and keep up with the top runners and just hope for the best. But on the last lap, in an effort to gain position and take the lead, Ron Clarke bumped Billy causing him to stumble and fall behind. For Billy Mills, the race and his hopes for victory appeared to be over. Even still, he kept telling himself, "I can win, I can win, I can win." As he pushed forward, he began to gain ground on the leaders.

When he crossed the finish line in first place, one of the event officials approached Billy and asked, "Who are you?" One of the greatest upsets in Olympic history had taken place that day.

Those who stumble and fall in a race oftentimes quit. As we strive to live like the Lord Jesus, there will be times that sin will trip us up and cause us to stumble. Here on this earth temptation and sin are real problems, and there will be times that we fail. But don't get discouraged and give up when you trip or stumble. Pray, ask for forgiveness and help, turn away from your sin, and try, try again.

Spread the Word

You will be my witnesses in Jerusalem, and in all Judea and Samaria, and to the ends of the earth.   Acts 1:8

It was April 18, 1775, and the British had planned a surprise attack. Their plot involved seizing the Patriot's weapons and arresting two of their leaders, Samuel Adams and John Hancock. There had been a growing resistance in the American colonies to British rule, trade laws and taxation. Earlier in 1773, a group of Patriots dressed as Indians, boarded British ships and dumped all of the tea overboard in an effort to protest the British tax on tea. One of the leaders of what became known as the Boston Tea Party was Paul Revere, a silversmith and businessman.

On the night of April 18, Revere received word from a stable boy who had overheard British soldiers talking of their plot. Revere then rowed across the river and mounted a horse. He somehow made his way safely through roads heavily guarded by the British and warned the towns of Lexington and Concord. Alerted by Revere that the British were on their way, Samuel Adams and John Hancock safely escaped and the American patriots prepared for battle. The battles that would take place marked the beginning of the Revolutionary War.

Every Christian has received an important message, which is the sacrificial death, burial and resurrection of the Lord Jesus. Through faith in Him, all the world can be saved. It is the mission of every Christian to take that message and share it with others. Paul writes in Romans 10:14, "And how can they believe in the one of whom they have not heard?" The answer of course is that they cannot believe in the message of Jesus if they haven't heard the message. Therefore, it is critical that we take the message we have received and share it wherever we go. Paul goes on to write in verse 15, "How beautiful are the feet of those who bring good news!"

Team !!!

... make my joy complete by being like-minded, having the same love, being one in spirit and purpose.   Philippians 2:2

Jimmy Durante was a great comedian of yesteryear. Because of his popularity and demanding schedule, he was a very busy man. Jimmy was once asked to speak before a group of World War II veterans. He agreed but informed the show's director that his performance must be short because afterwards he was scheduled to perform at a different location.

During the show for the war veterans Jimmy's short performance grew longer and longer. As it grew longer, the applause grew louder and louder. He just kept on staying. When Jimmy did take his final bow and left the stage he was asked, "What happened? Why did you stay?" Jimmy Durante pointed to two war veterans on the first row. One of the men had lost his left arm in the fighting, and the other man had lost his right. But together they had been able to clap and cheer on Jimmy Durante.

Now that's teamwork! That's cooperation!

God's work on earth is best accomplished through teamwork. A well organized team is always more effective than individual members working separately and alone. God calls us to be unified.

Members of a team accept each other's strengths and weaknesses. They then pull together and encourage one another to accomplish greater things than each member could ever accomplish alone. Don't forget; as Christians we are part of one big team, one big family, the Family of God.

Direction For Life

For this God is our God for ever and ever; he will be our guide even to the end.   Psalm 48:14

A World War II bomber had successfully flown a mission over enemy lines and was returning to its airfield to land. The plane was flying above the clouds and was pushed along by a powerful tailwind causing it to travel much faster than normal. When the instruments told the pilots to land, they looked at their watches and knew that it seemed too soon.

They faced a critical decision. If they believed their instruments, they would come down out of the clouds and prepare to land. But, to come down too soon might expose them to enemy fire. On the other hand, they could choose to trust their gut level feeling that it was too soon to land and remain above the clouds, hidden from enemy fire. But if the instruments were right, staying above the clouds meant overshooting their airfield and crashlanding because of a lack of fuel. Do they trust their instrument panel or their own feelings? They had to make a decision. They chose to ignore the instruments and trust their feelings. They stayed up and overshot the airfield. All crewmen died.

God created each of us and the universe in which we live. He knows us better than we know ourselves. In truth, God knows us perfectly. His love for us is great, and He desires to guide the course of our lives. And still the choice is ours to make. If we follow our personal feelings, wants and wishes, the result will be tragedy and destruction. But if we follow the direction and guidance of the living God of the universe, the end result will be reward and blessing.

The Way

I am the way, the truth, and the life. No man comes to the Father but by me. John 14:6

Once upon a time in a magnificent castle in the countryside there lived a man who was rich beyond imagination. With a portion of his wealth, he built a massive maze on his large estate. The maze stretched for miles; and the walls were very, very high. In the center, he placed a pot of gold. He then made his way into a poor village nearby. There he announced that any man who could find his way to the gold could have everything he could carry out. Each man left the village quickly and raced to the maze to find the riches in the center. Several days passed and finally a few of the men came out. When they did, they told terrible stories of some who had starved to death. Others went crazy from the endless passages, walls, and deadends.

A few days later, a young man stood quietly by the entrance of the maze. A stranger walked up beside the young man and asked, "Are you going into the maze alone?" He answered, "No, I'm afraid to go in alone. I have heard the stories of those who entered the maze and lived to tell of their horrible experiences." After a moment of silence the stranger replied, "Young man, I am the one who designed and built the maze. I know it like the back of my hand. I am the way. If you will follow me closely, I'll lead you right to the pot of gold."

"Follow me." Jesus spoke these two simple words time and time again to invite people into a close and personal relationship with Him. **JESUS IS THE WAY.** He is the way to abundant life on earth and eternal life in heaven. Following Jesus means trusting Him and living a life of obedience as we look to Him and imitate His example.

Perseverance Paid Off

Blessed is the man who perseveres under trial, because when he has stood the test, he will receive the crown of life that God has promised to those who love him.   James 1:12

Abraham Lincoln, the 16th President of the United States, was truly one of the greatest leaders of all time. He helped to abolish slavery and preserve the American Union during the Civil War.

But he persevered through one failure and hardship after another on his way to the presidency.

In 1831 his business failed.
In 1832 he was defeated for state legislature.
In 1833 another business failed.
In 1835 his business partner died leaving him in debt.
In 1835 the woman he was to marry died.
In 1836 he suffered a nervous breakdown.
In 1838 he was defeated for Speaker of the House.
In 1840 he was defeated for Elector.
In 1850 his son died.
In 1855 he was defeated for the Senate
In 1856 he was defeated running for Vice-President.
In 1858 he was again defeated for the Senate.

One of the realities of life is that hard times do come. Unfortunately, difficulties are often discouraging and set us back. Fortunately, though, difficulties also have a way of strengthening us and perfecting us. God can use them to prepare us for the future and the opportunities that lie ahead.

Real Faith

And without faith it is impossible to please God.   Hebrews 11:6

One day in 1860 a great crowd assembled at Niagara Falls to see the famous tightrope walker Blondin cross the raging falls. The wire was suspended 160 feet above the water and stretched almost 1,000 feet from the American side to the Canadian side. After successfully making the trip, he then pushed a wheelbarrow across the suspended wire as the people cheered their approval.

Blondin then asked the crowd if they believed he could take a person across in the wheelbarrow. They all shouted, "We believe, we believe!" He approached one of them and said, "Get in." But the man simply refused.

Though he was among those who said they believed, he wasn't willing to respond or to act on his words. He was obviously unwilling to commit and allow Blondin to take him across the falls. His faith was not real.

Faith is very important in the Christian life. It is by faith in Jesus Christ that we are saved from sin and become part of the family of God. It is also by faith that we live the Christian life day-by-day. But REAL FAITH is more than simply believing certain facts or truths. REAL FAITH involves trust, loyalty, and commitment. REAL FAITH is always active.

The Search

But seek first his kingdom and his righteousness, and all these things will be given to you as well.   Matthew 6:33

When the H.M.S. Titanic slipped out of the harbor in April 1912 for her maiden voyage, she was brand new and the largest and most luxurious passenger ship ever built. She was considered unsinkable and carried some of the most important and wealthy people of the day.

But just 5 days into her journey, the Titanic hit an iceberg and sank. She took with her over 1,500 of the 2,200 passengers and crew. For almost 75 years the Titanic rested 2 1/2 miles below the ocean's surface. There she lay undisturbed and undiscovered.

In 1985 Robert Ballard found her rusty remains. He had risked his life many times and spent millions of dollars during his 13 year search. Ballard had endured criticism and experienced numerous setbacks but at last, "mission accomplished." Finally, the search that had dominated so much of his life was over.

Our lives are like a treasure hunt. It seems that we all search for things to satisfy the deep needs and longings of our soul. Some people think that riches and possessions will satisfy. Others believe that success in sports, art, or music will make them happy. And then there are those who try friendships, popularity, or power. The list goes on and on.

While many of these pursuits are good, none is good enough to satisfy for long. Only Jesus can fill the emptiness of our souls. Our search for Him is never in vain. We are always rewarded in the end. In fact, He promised, "Seek and you will find."

Cast Away

Cast all your anxiety on him because he cares for you.   I Peter 5:7

The most famous American plane to emerge from World War II was the Memphis Belle. The B-17 bomber was named after the pilot's girlfriend, Margaret Polk of Memphis, Tennessee. The airplane earned the distinction of being the first B-17 to complete 25 successful missions over Europe without losing a single crew member and then return to the United States under its own power. The crew shot down eight enemy fighters and earned a total of 51 decorations. Damaged repeatedly in the 25 air raids, the Memphis Belle had seven engines, two wings, and a tail section replaced.

A major motion picture, *Memphis Belle*, dramatized the story of the bomber's 25th and final mission. After successfully bombing a German factory, the plane lost engine power after being hit by the enemy's ground attatck. To help keep the heavy bomber in the air the pilot ordered that all excess weight be thrown overboard. Guns, ammunitions and other unnecessary items were cast away to lighten the load. The Memphis Belle made history and landed successfully to the cheers of the U.S. ground crews.

There are times in our lives when we can't carry the load of our troubles and worries. They seem too difficult to handle and too heavy to bear. During times of trouble we need to cast them away to someone who is able to carry the load. That "someone" is Jesus Christ. He loves and cares for each of us and is more than able to carry even the heaviest load.

A Second Chance

Therefore, if anyone is in Christ, he is a new creation; the old has gone, the new has come!   2 Corinthians 5:17

Eleven year-old Darvin Miller of Wisconsin was playing on a frozen creek when the ice gave way sending him into the freezing water. It was thirty minutes before rescue workers found him and pulled his lifeless body from Duncan Creek. Darvin had no pulse, and his lungs were filled with water. But the rescuers worked feverishly to warm his body, empty the water from his lungs, and fill them with air. When the ambulance arrived at the hospital, the little boy was pronounced dead on arrival and was administered the last rites by a priest.

But almost two hours later the little drowning victim began showing signs of life as his body began unfreezing. Doctors and nurses stepped in, and C.P.R. was performed on the little boy's body. Incredibly, after just two weeks, Darvin Miller left the hospital to go home. His arms and legs were paralyzed, but within two years he was back to normal. Even though Darvin had been officially dead, he was living again. He had a second chance on life.

When a person places his faith in Jesus Christ as Savior and Lord, he also receives a second chance on life. He is "born again." This means that his sins are forgiven, and he is born into the family of God and the kingdom of heaven. There is a new beginning and a fresh start. Through God's help old habits of sin are left behind, and there is a change of life that involves following Christ in our attitude, actions and words. The Bible tells us that "he is a new creation; the old has gone, the new has come."

Rich Beyond Imagination

And my God will meet all your needs according to his glorious riches in Christ Jesus.   Philippians 4:19

In 1992 there were 101 billionaires ($1,000,000,000.) in the United States. Bill Gates, co-founder of MICROSOFT, a leader in the computer industry, was the youngest among these.

But perhaps the richest man of all time was King Solomon of ancient Israel. He inherited the throne from his father David. II Chronicles 9:22 states, "King Solomon was greater in riches and wisdom than all the other kings of the earth." The Bible tells us that he made gold and silver as common and plentiful as the stones in the street. Solomon owned 40,000 horses, 1,400 chariots, and a fleet of trading ships at sea. It is estimated that his personal income was 1/2 billion dollars per year ($500,000,000).

But the riches of Solomon pale in comparison to the wealth and riches of our God. He is rich beyond our imagination. Psalm 50:10 states that He owns the "cattle on a thousand hills." David writes in Psalm 24, "The earth is the LORD'S, and everything in it, the world, and all who live in it." Our God owns it all.

Though His riches are truly amazing, even more amazing is that He wants to give generously to His children. Though we are undeserving of His goodness and favor, it is His character to give and to give and to give. In fact, God's goodness seems to have no boundaries because even while we were still sinners, He gave the greatest gift of all - His only son - Jesus Christ.

Grace That Is Simply Amazing

It is by grace you have been saved, through faith.   Ephesians 2:8

John was born in 1725, the son of a dedicated Christian woman. His father, a sea captain, did not share his mother's faith and love for Christ. At seven, John's mother died, and he went to live with a relative. But he was treated so cruelly that he finally ran away and joined the Royal Navy. John later deserted the Navy and ran away to Africa, where he lived a life of sin as a slave trader.

Once, while on a slave ship bound for England, he broke into the ship's supply of rum and got drunk. John fell overboard and almost drowned, but an officer speared him with a harpoon and he was pulled to safety. A large scar on his thigh was a constant reminder of the sin that almost cost him his life.

Later on the same journey, during a terrible storm which threatened to sink the ship, John cried out to God as he remembered his godly mother and Bible verses he had been taught as a child. Trusting in Christ, he was saved from sin and became a Christian.

Formerly involved in the cruel business of the slave trade, he became one of the great preachers of his day in England. John Newton's life and experiences inspired him to write the now famous hymn:

> *Amazing Grace! how sweet the sound,*
> *That saved a wretch like me!*
> *I once was lost, but now am found;*
> *Was blind, but now I see.*

God's grace is the love and kindness that He shows to us even though we have not earned it nor deserve it. Even while we were sinners, God sent His only son to die in our place for our sins. Those who believe in Him receive forgiveness of sin, become part of the family of God, and inherit a home in heaven. Now that's grace. NO! That's "Amazing Grace."

"Never Give Up!"

I have fought the good fight, I have finished the race, I have kept the faith. II Timothy 4:7

During the early days of World War II only England stood against the powerful Nazi army of Hitler's Germany. Sir Winston Churchill had been elected Prime Minister of England just nine months after the war began in 1939. Even against what seemed to be overwhelming odds, Churchill refused to give in. He made the now famous statement, "I have nothing to offer but blood, toil, tears, and sweat." He inspired and cheered the nation on to eventual victory almost six years later.

Churchill was once asked back to his old school to speak to the student body. After being introduced, he stepped to the podium and said, "Never give up." Pausing for almost a minute, he said more boldly, "Never give up." After another pause, he pounded the podium and shouted, "NEVER, NEVER, NEVER, NEVER, NEVER GIVE UP!" Churchill then turned quietly and took his seat. It was the shortest speech he ever delivered, and yet it is perhaps his most memorable.

The Apostle Paul wrote two letters to the young pastor named Timothy. In each, he encouraged him to persevere and never give up. Paul had experienced many trials and struggles in his own life. More than once he was beaten and imprisoned. But no matter how difficult life became, he never gave up. He trusted in the promises of God and kept on sharing the good news of salvation through Jesus Christ. In the end, Paul was able to say, "I have fought the good fight, I have finished the race, I have kept the faith."

Strength For Survival

My soul is weary with sorrow; strengthen me according to your word. Psalm 119:28

It was May 8, 1966, and American Pilot James Ray was flying his 105 Thunderchief over enemy lines in North Vietnam. The events that followed were a nightmare. Ray was shot down and captured by the North Vietnamese. For weeks he was questioned and tortured. The pain and agony was so great that he often wished he had died in the crash.

He finally signed a confession and was placed alone in a prison cell. Pain racked his body, and the guilt of signing the confession flooded his soul. But then a whisper came from a nearby cell, "Hey, buddy." It was a fellow prisoner. As he knelt down to peer through the crack under his door, Ray heard the prisoner ask if he knew any Bible verses.

Ray began to quote Psalm 23, "The Lord is my shepherd..." As he did, the prisoner repeated each line until it was memorized. Other prisoners began to share Bible verses they had memorized as children.

As time passed, he and the other prisoners made ink from a mixture of water and brick dust and they wrote Bible verses on sheets of toilet paper. The sheets were then secretly passed from cell to cell. They knew that their actions were risky, but they also understood that God's Word was important to their survival. The living conditions in the prison seemed cruel and unbearable. But James Ray endured the countless hardships and was released after seven years of captivity.

The Bible is God's message of hope and help during the best and the worst of times. There is power within its pages. Therefore it is critical that we know the message that God has given to us in the Bible. To do so we must take the time each day to read it, study it, and allow it to become a part of our lives.

Hope For Tomorrow

But those who hope in the LORD will renew their strength.

Isaiah 40:31

Many years ago, 10-year-old Glen Cunningham and a friend mistakenly poured gasoline on a stove heater in their country schoolhouse. The explosion killed his friend and left Glen critically injured. His legs were so badly hurt that the doctors felt they should both be amputated. Hoping for a miracle, the parents begged to wait a day. The doctors reluctantly agreed. Stubborn hope kept them asking each day afterwards for just one more day. And each day the doctors gave in to the parent's wishes.

After several months, when the bandages were removed, Glenn's left leg was almost 2 1/2 inches shorter than his right. In addition, he was missing most of the toes on his right foot. The doctors regretfully informed the parents that he would never walk. But through hope and hard work, Glen not only walked again, he also ran. Oh, how he ran! He ran so fast that one day this 10-year-old survivor of a tragic accident would represent the United States in the Olympic Games and be known as the "world's fastest human being."

HOPE is the expectation of something good. When there is no hope, there is only discouragement, depression, and defeat. Someone once said, "If you can convince a man that there is no hope, he will curse the day he was born."

Fortunately, there is hope. When we hope in the Lord our attention is taken off our circumstances. Instead of being on our problems, our focus is on an almighty God and what He can do. Such hope turns defeat into perseverance and discouragement into enthusiasm. As long as we hope in the Lord we can confidently look forward to better days.

When Good Isn't Good Enough

He saved us, not because of righteous things we had done, but because of his mercy.   Titus 3:5

For years, John Wesley rose at 4 A.M. to spend two hours in prayer followed by another hour of Bible study. He would then spend the rest of the day, often late into the night, teaching and ministering within the prisons and hospitals.

Once, while sailing on a ship bound for England, a great storm arose. Giant waves and mighty winds threatened to sink the ship, and Wesley feared that he would die. Even though he had tirelessly served the Lord for many years he was unsure of what would happen to him if he died. He worried about where he would spend eternity.

Across the ship in the midst of the storm, Wesley heard a group of men singing hymns. He went over and asked, "How can you sing when this very night you are going to die?" The men responded, "If the ship goes down we will go up to be with the Lord forever." Wesley wondered how they could be so confident and why he did not have this kind of peace and assurance.

Fortunately for John Wesley the ship survived the storm. After making his way to London Wesley attended a church service and heard a sermon about "real saving faith." He realized that he had been wrong all along by trusting in his good works to save him and responded by placing his faith in Jesus Christ. John Wesley went on to become one of the greatest preachers of the 18th century.

Heaven is an eternal paradise - perfect and holy. But it is impossible to save yourself and gain entrance into heaven through anything you can do. In other words, you cannot work your way or earn your way into heaven. Our only hope is through faith in Jesus Christ and what He did when He died on the cross for our sins. As John Wesley discovered, the end result of such saving faith is a wonderful sense of peace - not fear.

No Greater Love

Greater love has no one than this, that he lay down his life for his friends.   John 15:13

Two teenagers, Malcolm and Barbara, were enjoying a hike in Glacier National Park when Malcolm noticed a stirring in the brush ahead. Moving closer to get a better look he smiled as he saw two small bear cubs wrestling playfully. But his joy was interrupted when Barbara screamed from behind him, scaring off the two young cubs. Malcolm turned to see an 800-pound grizzly bear, the mother of the cubs, emerge and begin chasing Barbara. Rising up on its hind legs, the enormous beast lashed out, knocking her to the ground. She screamed hysterically as blood gushed from her forehead.

Malcolm stood frozen for a moment but then reached for his hunting knife. Without thinking of his own safety, he ran to the bear, leaped upon the beast's back and began stabbing it in the neck. But with one sweep of its paw, Malcolm was knocked to the ground, and his knife sailed into the brush. The bear, now turning her attention to Malcolm, clamped down on his head with her mighty steel jaws. Malcolm tried to free himself only to have the bear slam his arm to the ground with her forepaw breaking his arm in two places. The beast then bit into his shoulder and shook him from side to side like a rag doll.

When she finally released him, Malcolm lay still, almost losing consciousness. The mother bear then stepped over what appeared to be his lifeless body and disappeared into the brush. Barbara ran for over an hour to get help. When a helicopter finally arrived to airlift him to the hospital, only a faint pulse could be detected. Malcolm miraculously recovered though he lost an eye and underwent almost two years of reconstructive surgeries.

Aware of the danger, and yet risking his life to save Barbara's, Malcolm was given the CIVILIAN MEDAL OF HONOR. Inscribed on the medal are the words of Jesus Christ from

John 15:13: "Greater love has no man than this, that a man lay down his life for a friend."

According to Jesus the second greatest commandment is to "love your neighbor as yourself." Real love is more than a warm, fuzzy feeling. Real love is active and proves and demonstrates itself through both actions and words. Jesus emphasized that the greatest love is a sacrificial love and gives the very best for the good of another.

Seeing Christ In Christians

"Follow me," Jesus said to him.   Luke 5:27

Mahatma Gandhi, the great leader of the Hindu religion, is honored as the father of the nation of India. Through a unique method of nonviolent resistance, Gandhi helped free India from British rule. Earlier in his life he spent almost 21 years in South Africa after studying law in London. During his time there, Gandhi often attended church. He often read the Bible and later admitted to being attracted to Jesus Christ. And yet Gandhi never became a Christian.

While in South Africa he observed those who attended church. It seemed that some went simply out of habit. Others went to church because of friends and family. And there were those who went only because of the activites and events that were offered. It was as if church was a recreational activity just like anything else.

The Christians he saw appeared no different than non-Christians. Gandhi confessed: "I have the highest admiration for the Christian life and the Christ of the Bible. And I might have become a Christian if I could have seen one."

People everywhere were drawn to Jesus during His earthly life. They were attracted to Him because He was so different. They couldn't help but notice His great love and kindness. They saw Him feed the hungry, comfort the hurting, heal the sick and even raise the dead.

The Christian life is a life of following Jesus Christ. As we follow Jesus and others see His love and kindness in us, they will be drawn to Him. How sad that Gandhi saw no one in the church that resembled Christ. And because of this, it appears that he was "turned off," never believed and never received forgiveness and eternal life.

Finishing Well

I have finished the race.   II Timothy 4:7

One of history's greatest battles took place in 490 B.C. when only 7,000 Greek soldiers defeated 20,000 invading Persians outside the Greek city of Marathon. Following the battle, a runner was sent all the way to Athens to share the good news of the great victory. When he finally reached the city he shouted, "We are Victorious!" Then the runner collapsed and died. Such were the beginnings of the Marathon, a 26.2 mile endurance race.

More than 2,000 years later, the marathon was run at the 1968 Olympics in Mexico City. Mamo Wolde of Ethiopia won the gold medal. But perhaps the greatest drama took place more than an hour later with only a few spectators remaining in the stadium. The last runner in the marathon entered the stadium, bloodied and bandaged from a fall. His name was John Stephen Akhwari, and he painfully hobbled around the track and across the finish line. The small crowd roared as if he had been the winner. Akhwari was asked why he endured such pain and didn't quit when he obviously had no chance of winning. His reply is now famous, "I don't think you understand. My country did not send me to Mexico City to start the race. They sent me to finish the race."

The Bible compares the Christian life to a race. We begin the race by placing our faith in Jesus Christ. The race continues as each day of our lives we follow the example of Jesus and live a life of faith and obedience. The race ends as we breathe our last breath in this world and Jesus receives us into the kingdom of heaven. God's desire is that we run the race, never give up, and finish well.

Encouragement

Do not let any unwholesome talk come out of your mouths, but only what is helpful for building others up. Ephesians 4:29

Ben was the worst student in the fifth grade at Higgins Elementary School. No one else even came close. On one particular math quiz, he scored a zero out of 30. He was called "dummy" by his fellow classmates and became the subject of their jokes and laughter. It is no wonder that he began to believe that he truly was stupid and that the bottom of the class was where he belonged.

But Ben's mother did not accept what everyone else seemed to be saying about him. She refused to give up on her son and became a source of hope and encouragement in the midst of failure and criticism. Limiting the number of hours that he could watch television, his mother initiated a disciplined course of study at home that would help him improve his grades.

His grades almost immediately began to go up, and Ben went on to rank third in his graduating class. After attending Yale University on academic scholarship, he went on to medical school and became a brain surgeon. In 1987 newspapers all over the world reported that Siamese twins connected at the head had been successfully separated by Dr. Ben Carson. The twins miraculously survived.

Dr. Ben Carson gives much of the credit for his success to the loving words and encouragement of his dear mother. He admits that if it hadn't been for her he might have given up as a fifth grader at Higgins Elementary.

Our words have power. And because they have the power to hurt and destroy, God commands us to be careful and keep a tight reign on our tongues. We are to let absolutely nothing that is harmful come out of our mouths. On the other hand, words also have the ability to encourage and empower others to do the extraordinary. Therefore, be generous with words of kindness and praise.

Impossible?

For nothing is impossible with God.   Luke 1:37

Dave Dravecky was at the top of his game. As a starting pitcher for the San Francisco Giants he had earned a place in the record books by pitching almost 20 innings during the postseason without giving up a single run. His honors included pitching in an All-Star Game, two National League Championships and a World Series.

He was unaware that the growing lump on the shoulder of his pitching arm was anything that should concern him. Dave noticed it in the fall of 1987 but within a year it had grown to the size of a golf ball. Biopsies later revealed that the lump was cancer. He was then told by specialists that half of his shoulder muscle would need to be removed along with the tumor. When Dave asked about his future as a pitcher, the doctors said that his chances of returning to professional baseball were zero. Their hopes were that he would someday be able to toss the ball with his kids in the backyard.

But Dave was not discouraged nor did he feel sorry for himself. He believed in an Almighty God. His faith and courage kept him going during the surgery and the grueling workouts in the months that followed. Ten months afterwards, he did what the doctors said could not be done. Dave Dravecky pitched eight innings for the Giants and beat the Cincinatti Reds 4-3.

Our God never changes. He is the same God who created the heavens and the earth in only six days. Nothing is impossible for Him. He is able to do more than we can ask or imagine. Our problems, big and small, are simply opportunities for our God to demonstrate His power and glory. As we pray to Him, trust in Him and obey Him, God is more than able to help us in our time of need. He will either change our problem or equip us to meet the challenge of that problem.

Trading Places

But God demonstrated his own love for us in this: While we were still sinners, Christ died for us. Romans 5:8

No twins ever looked more alike than Martin and Morgan. Their mother even had trouble telling them apart. But while they were identical in appearance, they were opposite in their actions. Martin was a good boy. He repectfully obeyed his parents and teachers, took pride in his schoolwork, and was popular with classmates. Morgan was an entirely different story. He stayed in trouble. It was almost as if he had no conscience at all. As Morgan grew, so did his trouble. While Martin was an absolute joy to his parents, their hearts were broken over their son Morgan.

Eventually Morgan committed murder and was sentenced by the courts to die in the electric chair. On the eve of his death, Martin came to visit his twin brother in prison. When the guard left them alone, Martin took off his clothes and instructed his twin to do the same. Martin then put on Morgan's prison uniform and told Morgan to dress in his street clothes. When their visit was over, the guard came and escorted Morgan to freedom, never realizing that a switch had taken place. The next day, Martin took his brother's place in the electric chair and was put to death. In the days that followed, Morgan could not forget the price his brother had paid to set him free. He also realized that he had an important decision to make. He could either continue his life of crime or he had the opportunity to start afresh and live a life like his brother, Martin.

The Bible clearly tells us that each of us has sinned and that our sin deserves punishment according to God's holy law. But God's love for us is so awesome that while we were still sinners, Jesus took our place and died for us. Though He was perfectly innocent, Jesus willingly became our substitute and received the punishment that we deserved.Through faith in Him our sins are forgiven and we have the opportunity to start afresh.

A Higher Authority

Your word is a lamp to my feet and a light for my path.

Psalm 119:105

In the black of the night only a dim light shone in the distance. As the ship's captain looked out across the ocean with his telescope, it seemed that they were on a collision course with another ship. He ordered the first mate to send out a message to the light he saw in the ship's path: "Alter your course by 10 degrees south." A reply quickly came from the distant light: "Alter your course 10 degreees to the north." Thinking that his command had been disregarded, the captain of the ship had a new message sent: "Alter your course by 10 degrees south, I am the captain!" A reply came back: "Alter your course 10 degrees north, I am a seaman third class."

Shocked at the nerve of the young sailor, the captain was furious that his two previous messages had gone unheeded. He sent a third and final message that he knew would strike fear in the heart of this impudent sailor: "Young man, I can have you court-martialed. I order you to alter your course immediately 10 degrees to the south! I am a battleship!" A chilling reply came back to the captain from the light ahead: "With all due respect, I command you to alter your course by 10 degrees to the north! I am a lighthouse!"

Our highest authority is God and He has communicated His plan and purpose for man within the pages of the Bible. God's Word is like a lighthouse that guides and directs. Just as a ship should alter its course according to the lighthouse, so we must also alter our lives according to the guiding light of God's Word. Yet many people rebel against God and choose their own course through life. By doing so, they put themselves on a collision course with discipline, confusion, pain and heartache. On the other hand, those who submit to God's authority and follow His directions will always be rewarded and blessed.

It Just Doesn't Matter

What good is it for a man to gain the whole world, yet forfeit his own soul?   Mark 8:36

"Pistol" Pete Maravich was a basketball legend in his own time. He amazed fans with his behind-the-back passes, between-the-leg dribbles and his ability to score at will. The "Pistol" finished his college career at LSU by being named "Player of the Year" in 1970. As a three-time All-American, he had become the top scorer in college basketball history. Later as a professsional, he averaged 24.2 points per game and once scored 68 points in a game.

But it was not until 1982, after his retirement, that Pete Maravich became a Christian. He later admitted to a former coach that his desire was to be remembered as a good Christian, a good husband, and a good father. Speaking at a Billy Graham Crusade in front of 35,000 people , Pete stated: "Next week I'll be inducted into the Hall of Fame. I wouldn't trade my position in Christ for a thousand NBA championships, for a thousand Hall of Fame rings or for a hundred billion dollars." Just a few months later, at the youthful age of 40, "Pistol" Pete Maravich unexpectedly died after playing basketball with some friends.

There are many who spend their entire lives chasing after the things of this world. But more important than fame and fortune is the forgiveness and eternal life that we receive through faith in Jesus Christ. When our life on this earth ends, little else will matter. Jesus asked the question: "What good is it for a man to gain the whole world, yet forfeit his own soul?" Of course the answer is that the whole world is worth absolutely nothing if a man is separated from God and the kingdom of heaven.

Standing Firm

Be strong and very courageous.   Joshua 1:7

While serving as a missionary to the Chinese, Lottie Moon heard pounding at her door during the New Year festivities in 1890. When she answered it she saw a group of new Christians from a local church that had just recently formed. They were uncontrollably upset. When they could finally speak they told her of the tragic events they had just witnessed.

During a family celebration a fellow-Christian had been tied, strung to a pole, and beaten by his own relatives for not joining them in their custom of worshipping their ancestors. For the same reason, another Christian had also been beaten by his brothers and dragged by his pigtail until it finally tore the scalp from his head.

Lottie Moon immediately traveled to the village where she found the group of frightened Christians and an angry crowd. Firmly standing her ground in front of the church, she addressed the crowd, "If you attempt to destroy this church, you will have to kill me first. Jesus gave His life for us Christians. Now I am ready to die for Him." Seeing the courage of the small woman, one by one the angry crowd turned away. One of the men came back to Lottie Moon and said, "Please, I would like to know more about this Jesus who gives such courage."

Many misunderstand courage and think that it is the absence of fear. As Christians, the courage we receive through the presence and promises of Christ allows us to face our fears and master them. It means standing up for what we know is right in spite of our fears. It involves taking risks when we know the risk is worthwhile. Such courage is noticed by others and in turn inspires others to also stand up.

Surprise Attack

Put on the full armor of God so that you can take your stand against the devil's schemes.   Ephesians 6:11

It was a quiet and beautiful Sunday morning at Pearl Harbor, the U.S. navy base located in the Hawaiian Islands. But the events that unfolded on December 7, 1941, would change the course of world history. Suddenly, just before 8 A.M., the Japanese struck without warning. When Commander Fuchida radioed, "Tora, tora, tora!", Japanese bombs fell from the sky like rain. Caught by surprise, 231 American planes were parked wing-tip to wing-tip on the ground below. Ninety-six helpless American ships sat anchored in the harbor like sitting ducks.

One violent explosion blasted the battleship *Arizona,* instantly killing 1,000 American sailors. Some of the bodies were literally rocketed through the air. Many were covered with oil and burned to death while others lay wounded and dying in the waters. The bombing continued for two hours, destroying ships, planes, oil tanks and airplane hangars. Nearly 4,000 Americans were killed or wounded in the surprise attack.

The next day President Roosevelt appeared before congress and sounded a call for Americans to fight. In one month over 60,000 Americans volunteered to fight in World War II. The fighting ended almost four years later on September 2, 1945 with American and Allied forces victorious.

Schemes, lies, trickery and deceit are the tools and strategy of Satan. I Peter 5:8 describes Satan as a "roaring lion looking for someone to devour." He desires to attack us when we least expect it and utterly destroy us when we are weak. Therefore it is very important that we never drop our guard or underestimate the reality and power of Satan.

Tough Love

Be kind and compassionate to one another, forgiving each other, just as in Christ God forgave you.   Ephesians 4:32

Corrie ten Boom and her entire family were arrested by the Germans and sent to a Nazi concentration camp during World War II. When the Germans occupied Holland and began arresting Jews, the ten Boom family had felt it their Christian responsiblity to help those in need. They each risked their lives and safety by hiding Jews in a secret room that was built behind Corrie's bedroom on the top floor of the family home. In the end, however, they were betrayed by a spy and arrested for aiding the Jews.

Conditions in the concentration camp were horrid. The barracks were filled with wooden platforms that were covered with dirty, stinking hay that was crawling with fleas. Each of the prisoners worked an 11-hour day. Meals consisted of black bread for breakfast and turnip soup for supper. Only Corrie and a brother survived the experience.

When the war was finally over, Corrie shared her story and her message of God's love all over the world. On one occasion, after speaking to a church in Germany, she was confronted by one of the Nazi guards that had treated her and the other prisoners so cruelly. Her own sister had died as the result of such treatment. The man had since become a Christian and was now asking for forgiveness. Corrie stood frozen and silent. Realizing that God had forgiven her own sin, she prayed for help, shook his hand and said, "I do forgive you, brother. With all my heart."

It was while you and I were guilty that Jesus willingly took our punishment, suffered and died for our sins. Yet, while He was on that cruel cross, He prayed, "Father, forgive them, for they do not know what they are doing." Now that is TOUGH LOVE! Motivated by the love of Jesus and His forgiveness to each of us, we should respond by loving and forgiving others.

Pressing On

I press on toward the goal to win the prize. Philippians 3:14

At the 1972 Olympics, the favorites to win the gold medal in the 10,000 meter run were Dave Bedford of Great Britain and Emiel Puttemans of Belgium. Both runners had broken the Olympic record in their qualifying races. Little was expected from 23-year-old Lasse Viren of Finland who placed fourth in his qualifying heat. Near the halfway point of the race no one was surprised to see Bedford in the lead. Puttemans was in fourth, followed by Viren.

Suddenly and unexpectedly Viren tripped and fell. Fortunately, he was not trampled by the other runners and he quickly got to his feet. Even still, Viren was now more than 50 meters behind because of his fall. With half of the race still to be run, he did not give up, but instead sprinted after the other contestants. Viren soon caught up with the front runners. He then took the lead and held off a late charge by Puttemans to win the gold medal. Lasse Viren had run one of the greatest races in Olympic history.

Every athlete faces problems, hardships, and even failures. Those who quit will never experience success or victory. This is also true in the Christian life. Problems, hardships, and failure are to be expected. Paul's strategy for success is given in Philippians 3:13-14. "But one thing I do: Forgetting what is behind and straining toward what is ahead, I press on toward the goal to win the prize for which God has called me heavenward in Christ Jesus."

Evidence Of Our Love

If you love me, you will obey what I command.   John 14:15

Perhaps the greatest military leader who ever lived was Alexander the Great. On one particular campaign, he and a small group of soldiers approached an enemy city that was protected by a massive wall of stone. Atop the wall was a great army ready for battle. Alexander confidently approached the city and shouted, "I demand to see the king." When he appeared, Alexander commanded, "Surrender immediately."

The king burst forth in laughter and then shouted, "This wall cannot be penetrated and you are greatly outnumbered. Why should I surrender to you?" Alexander replied, "Allow me to show you."

He then ordered his men to line up and march directly toward a cliff that dropped hundreds of feet to the rocky landing below. When the first of Alexander's soldiers approached the cliff he marched off the edge to his death. In shock and disbelief, the king watched as the second, third and fourth did the same. Alexander then ordered the men to halt and return to his side as the king and his soldiers watched atop the wall. Realizing that he could never win a battle against an army of men who were so completely committed to their leader, the king promptly surrendered to Alexander the Great.

How much more should you and I be committed to obeying the commands of the King of Kings and Lord of Lords who loves us more than we can even imagine. For the Christian, obedience is simply doing what Jesus says. It is not always easy but it is always necessary. Obedience is the real test of our love and loyalty to King Jesus.

Tragedy to Triumph

And we know that in all things God works for the good of those who love Him, who have been called according to His purpose.

Romans 8:28

Joni Eareckson Tada is an accomplished artist, author, singer, recording artist, and world-reknowned conference speaker. She has also starred in a movie about her life and experiences. Joni is also bound to a wheelchair. A diving accident at the age of 17 broke her neck and left her paralyzed. She would never again be able to move her arms or legs.

For months her life hung in balance. She endured many long and painful months in the hospital. Unable to eat because of nausea, her weight dropped from 125 to 80 pounds. Feeling homesick, bored and hopeless, Joni simply wanted to die. Her life had been permanently changed. She could no longer perform even the simplest tasks. What did she have to offer God?

But as time passed, Joni began to understand that God had not forgotten her. He still loved and cared for her just as before the accident. She began to accept her obvious physical limitations but also trusted in a God who is unlimited in His ability to overcome such limitations. In spite of her disability, God was at work in her life to do something good and worthwhile. Joni developed new talents and abilities in spite of her weaknesses. As a result, her life and experiences are a source of inspiration and hope to millions around the world.

Jesus once fed 5,000 hungry people with just 5 loaves of bread and 2 fish (Luke 9:10-17). In much the same way Jesus is able to take a person's life that is freely given to Him, multiply it and accomplish more than we could ever imagine. Through His unlimited power and resources, He is able to overcome our weaknesses and produce something good.

Help for the Needy

Let us not become weary in doing good, for at the proper time we will reap a harvest if we do not give up.   Galatians 6:9

Mayor LaGuardia of New York once visited a night court in the poorest area of the city. After dismissing the judge on duty, the mayor took the bench and prepared to hear the next case before him. A poor old woman was being charged with stealing a loaf of bread. Defending herself, she stated before the court, "My daughter's husband has left the family. My daughter is sick and the children are starving." The store owner refused to drop the charges against the old woman and insisted that she be punished in order to set an example for others in the neighborhood.

The mayor then turned to the woman and sighed, "I must punish you. I can make no exceptions, the law has been broken. Ten dollars or 10 days in jail." But even as he was pronouncing the poor woman's sentence, he took 10 dollars out of his wallet and threw it into a hat. Mayor LaGuardia then stated to the room full of people, "Here's the 10 dollar fine and I'm going to fine everyone in the courtroom 50 cents for living in a city where a woman must steal to feed her hungry grandchildren." The bailiff collected the fines and was then instructed to turn them over to the accused woman. A New York newspaper reported the next day that $47 were given to a poor old woman who stood accused of stealing bread in order to feed her grandchildren.

We live in a world full of needs. People with a variety of needs are all around us. Most of us have so much that we could give - time, love, attention, encouragement, money and other resources. Yet the sad reality is that we often don't do those things that we could to improve the life of someone else. Jesus was very clear to communicate to His followers that doing good to those in need is the same as doing it unto Him.

Thank God!!!

Give thanks to the LORD for He is good. His love endures forever.
Psalm 136:1

On September 1620, a dedicated group of Christians set sail on an overcrowded ship called the Mayflower to set up a colony in the "Promised Land." They named this new colony Plymouth and elected William Bradford as their governor.

Almost three years later in the summer of 1623, there had been no rain for almost seven weeks. The brook was shrinking day-by-day, and the crops they had planted in the spring were dying in the fields. The survival of the colony was at stake and weighed heavily upon the governor's shoulders.

Trusting that God alone had the power to send rain, Bradford declared a day of fasting and prayer. On that day, every resident of Plymouth gathered at the town's meeting house where they sang hymns, read Scripture and prayed until sundown. As he left, William Bradford looked at the sky to see the clouds gathering. During the night, when the rain began to fall, he thanked the Lord, knowing that the rains meant all the difference in their survival as a colony.

We often forget to thank others for acts of goodness toward us. Even worse, we often forget to thank God. The Bible reminds us in James 1:17 that "Every good and perfect gift is from above, coming down from the Father." It is good for each of us to look for and see the goodness of God all around us, for He alone is the creator and sustainer of all things. Our God rightly deserves our thanks as the one who gives "every good and perfect gift."

Mission Not Accomplished

For the Son of Man came to seek and to save what was lost.

Luke 19:10

On the night of April 15, 1912, a giant iceberg tore a 300 foot hole in the side of the Titanic as it crossed the Atlantic on its maiden voyage. The Titanic was thought to be "unsinkable" and was not adequately equipped with enough lifeboats for the number of passengers and crew members aboard. When the 20 lifeboats were launched from the now sinking ship, they were only partly filled with passengers.

Two hours and 40 minutes after striking the iceberg, the Titanic sank to the ocean floor approximately 12,000 feet below. She carried with her hundreds who were still on board. Many others were left in the icy waters of the Atlantic, struggling to stay alive.

One of the lifeboats did go back in an effort to seek and save those who cried for help. A few were saved. Sadly, no other boat joined in the effort to rescue those who were still alive. Yet many of the lifeboats were only half-filled. Still they rowed a safe distance away from the cries of those who were drowning. Each feared to go back and risk the possibility of being overturned by the many who desperately needed help.

Jesus stated in Luke 19:10 that His mission was "to seek and to save what was lost." When we trust in Jesus and He saves us from our sins, we become His representatives, and His mission becomes our mission. Sadly, we are often like the Titanic lifeboats and fail to do the very thing for which we were created. When we fail to share His love and message and we fail to live out the Christian life on earth, we fail to carry out the very purpose and mission for which we were saved.

For the Team

Then make my joy complete by being like-minded, having the same love, being one in spirit and purpose. Philippians 2:2

The Japanese men's gymnastics team suffered a severe blow in the 1976 Olympics when Shun Fujimoto broke his kneecap while competing in the floor excercise. The team scores were close at the time, and Japan's main competition for the gold medal was the Soviet Union. Fujimoto was one of the strongest athletes on the Japanese team and was concerned that news of his injury would only worry his coaches and teammates. So for the good of the team, he not only remained in the competition but also kept it a secret.

Though his kneecap was broken, Fujimoto endured the pain and scored well in the following event which was the pommel horse. His next event was the rings and he performed brilliantly. He knew that only the dismount and landing awaited. He also knew that landing on the mat with such force would be excruciating. After landing and holding his position for the required time in front of the judges, his knee gave way. Fujimoto received an incredible 9.7 out of a possible 10.

Unfortunately he had injured the knee further. Japanese officials and teammates were now aware of his injury and would no longer allow him to continue in the competition. But inspired by Fujimoto and his unselfish commitment to the overall team, the Japanese went on to win the gold medal. They dedicated their win to their fallen teammate Shun Fujimoto.

As Christians we are all part of one team called the Church or the body of Christ. It is the desire of God that we be unified - having the same purpose, same spirit, and same direction. To do so we must be less concerned with our own needs and more concerned about the needs of the team. By unselfishly pulling together, we can do greater things than we could ever do on our own. Together we can accomplish God's work here on earth.

Hope Through Encouragement

Therefore encourage one another and build each other up.

I Thessalonians 5:11

As a boy LeRoy Butler was so severely "pigeon-toed" that his feet almost pointed to one another. As a result, numerous operations were performed in an effort to correct the bones in his feet. Doctors would break the "crooked" bones, straighten them and then apply casts. After proper healing, this procedure would then be repeated. LeRoy confessed that he lost count of the number of surgeries. During these years he spent much of his time in a wheelchair because of the weakness and pain in his legs.

LeRoy just wanted to be like everyone else and even dreamed of someday playing football in the NFL. Others laughed when he dared to speak of his dream. But not his mother. She encouraged LeRoy and helped him stay focused during those difficult days. While his friends played football, LeRoy could only watch ... dream ... and hope.

Finally at the age of 12, he was able to suit up and compete with his friends. During his first season LeRoy wore special steel supports on his once crooked feet. He still remembers intercepting a pass in one game only to trip over his own feet and fumble. But through the encouragement of his mother LeRoy persevered and before long was the star of his high school football team. He went on to earn a scholarship to play for Florida State University and years later would help the Green Bay Packers win the Super Bowl.

Circumstances often hinder us from seeing the gifts and opportunities that God has given to each of us. Circumstances can also hinder us from reaching our goals until sometime in the future. But encouragement from others can help us to persevere and accomplish more than we ever dreamed possible - in spite of our circumstances. Therefore, God's Word instructs each of us to "encourage one another."

Determined to Live by Faith

Abraham believed the LORD, and He credited it to him as righteousness. Genesis 15:6

A man by the name of Christopher wrote in his journal of a vision that he believed to be inspired by God - to sail west into the Atlantic Ocean and discover a new trade route to the riches of the Indies. To the scientists and navigators and the wise and powerful men of his day - it seemed like the dream of a fool. The king of Portugal said NO. King Henry of England said NO. King Charles of France said NO.

But determined to live by faith, Christopher did not give up so easily. For seven long years he waited and prayed and sought the will of God. In the spring of 1492, his faith paid off and the king and queen of Spain agreed to finance his voyage. On August 3rd, he set sail. More than two months later, the weary crew anchored and set foot on an island they named San Salvador which means "Holy Savior." Christopher was certain that God had guided him to Asia, not realizing the greater discovery he had made. Christopher Columbus had found a new world - America.

Approximately 3,600 years before, a man by the name of Abraham packed his few belongings and left his country, his family, his friends, his way of life, and the comforts of home. It seemed foolish. His actions defied rational thought. Not knowing the where, nor the how, nor the when, Abraham set out. But it is very important to understand - God had spoken. God had given him a commandment to go and a vision and a promise of the future. By faith, Abraham obeyed.

Today, Abraham stands out as a landmark of faith and obedience. He uttered no prophecy, wrote no book, sang no song, gave no law. Yet the Bible speaks of him alone as "the father of the faithful" and "the friend of God." Surely there is no greater honor.

The Value of God's Word

All Scripture is God-breathed and is useful for teaching, rebuking, correcting and training in righteousness, so that the man of God may be thoroughly equipped for every good work. II Timothy 3:16

Andrew joined the Dutch army looking for thrills and adventure. Shipped off to the East Indies, he found that the people he was fighting only wanted their freedom from Dutch rule. Andrew was miserable. When he wasn't taking unnecessary risks during the fighting, he tried to numb his mind and emotions with alcohol.

After being shot in the ankle, he was recovering in the hospital when he began to read the Bible from cover to cover. Soon afterwards, Andrew trusted in Christ and then began to sense God's direction to be involved in missions. During the 1950's several European countries were being ruled by ungodly and communist governments that did not allow religious freedom. Andrew learned while visiting these countries that there were precious few Bibles. In some churches, the pastor did not even have one.

So Brother Andrew began to smuggle Bibles illegally into these countries where churches were struggling. When he approached border checkpoints, he would pray that God would make seeing eyes blind and they would be unable to see the Bibles that he had hidden in his luggage or automobile. Brother Andrew continued this work of providing Bibles to Christians in communist countries eventually expanding his work in Europe to also include China, Cuba, and Africa.

The famous preacher, Dwight L. Moody, once said, "In prayer we talk to God. In Bible study, God talks to us, and we had better let God do most of the talking." There is no way to place a value on the Bible because its value is both infinite and eternal. As we read the Bible, "God talks to us" and teaches us His plan and purpose for our lives. Therefore, open your Bible, read it, study it, memorize it, think about it, and most importantly - obey it.

"Free at Last"

It is for freedom that Christ has set us free.   Galatians 5:6

Jon Kregel played professional soccer on the same team as the legendary Pele. But unable to handle his success as a soccer pro and in an effort to fill the emptiness that he felt inside, Jon descended down a road of money, sex, alcohol, and drugs. He smuggled drugs and saw thousands of dollars change hands in drug deals. He watched in horror as his own partner was rolled out of a car after being murdered by other drug dealers.

Finally arrested for the possession and delivery of cocaine, Jon was sentenced to a prison in Huntsville, Texas. Sitting alone in a prison cell at the very lowest point in his life, he found what he had been searching for all along. He realized that it was God he needed. So, kneeling next to his prison bed, Jon prayed for forgiveness of his sins and invited Jesus into that lonely place in his heart.

Jon Kregel admits that even though he was locked in a prison cell, for the first time in his entire life, he truly felt free. Since his release in 1987, he has traveled the world sharing his message of Good News to thousands in schools and churches.

Jesus stated in John 8:34, "I tell you the truth, everyone who sins is a slave to sin." The Good News is that Jesus, the Son of God, died for our sins. He took our place on the cross and suffered our punishment even though He was innocent. Through faith in Jesus, we are set free. We are freed from the condemnation or penalty of sin which is eternal separation from God in a place called "Hell." But we are also set free from the power of our old sinful desires. We are finally able to obey God.

Meeting Needs

Your attitude should be the same as that of Christ Jesus.

Philippians 2:5

As a young nun living in India, Teresa's heart went out to those living in the slums that were beyond the convent walls where she lived. Many were hungry and homeless, diseased and dying. Abandoned children walked the streets. Aborted babies were found still alive behind the hospital. Approximately 30,000 in the city of Calcutta suffered from leprosy, and no one seemed to be helping them.

Her deeply religious mother had taught Teresa as a child to care for the poor. She realized that to help these people she really needed to live among them. She received permission from the Pope and in 1950 formed the Missionaries of Charity, a new order which would live and minister to the poorest of the poor.

But not everyone appreciated her work. On one occasion a policeman was sent by Hindu and Muslim neighbors to kick the nuns out of their home for those who were dying. But when he saw Mother Teresa picking worms from the open wounds of a dying man while speaking words of comfort, the policeman left. He had witnessed the love of Christ in action.

WWJD. These letters appear on t-shirts, caps, necklaces, bumper stickers, etc. This popular slogan stands for "What Would Jesus Do?" The question is meant to emphasize the importance of responding to every situation in the way that Jesus would if He were in our shoes. Everything about us - our attitudes, actions, and words - are to be like Jesus. He responded to people in need with love and kindness. We are challenged to do the same.

Honoring Our Commitments

Be on your guard; stand firm in the faith; be men of courage; be strong.   I Corinthians 16:13

Eric was a "natural" athlete. He captained the boarding school's cricket team, won numerous awards in rugby and set several records in track and field. He later played rugby for Edinburgh University and the national team from Scotland. But of all the sports, running was Eric's favorite. Winning races throughout the British Empire, people everywhere began to take notice of his blazing speed. In 1924, he traveled to Paris for the Olympic Games. At the age of 22 Eric became Britain's greatest hope for a gold medal in the 100 meter race.

But when he received the schedule for his race Eric refused to run because the event was to be held on Sunday. The idea of racing on the "Lord's Day" was unthinkable for Eric because he had made a decision long before to rest from work and sports and to honor God on Sundays. Many of his countrymen considered him a traitor for refusing to run, and newspapers criticized him for his decision. But Eric would not compromise his commitment and instead began preparing for the 400 meters, a race that was clearly not his strongest distance.

Just before the 400 meter race, one of Eric's trainers slipped him a note with a verse from the Bible that said, "He that honors me, I will honor." When the race was over, the winner and new world record holder was Eric Liddell. The earlier criticism and anger by his countrymen turned to respect and admiration, not only because he had won the gold medal for Britain, but because he was a man of uncompromising commitment to God.

It is not always easy to be courageous and stand up for what we believe. Sometimes it is not popular with others. But as followers of Jesus Christ our desire should be to please God and not men. Our faithfulness to Him is sometimes rewarded in the present, sometimes in the future. But our God is loving and faithful and He always honors and blesses our commitment and obedience. The LORD declares: "Those who honor me I will honor" (I Samuel 2:30).

Abundant Living

Jesus answered, "I am the way and the truth and the life."

John 14:6

David Robinson seemed to have it all. He was very intelligent and could master anything he set his mind to learn. A genius with computers and electronics, by himself he put together a wide screen television from a kit when he was only 15. He finished high school scoring an amazing 1320 on the SAT and then earned a degree from one of the nation's finest colleges, the Naval Academy. He could play the piano, saxophone and guitar and had "jammed" with some of the world's greatest jazz musicians. He had become an All-American basketball player as a junior in college. As a senior, David led the nation in blocked shots, ranked third in scoring and fourth in rebounding on his way to becoming college player of the year.

When he signed with the San Antonio Spurs in 1987, he received a 10-year contract worth $26 million, making him the richest basketball player in NBA history. He had five cars, two homes and more money than he could spend. On the court, his success continued by winning All-Star and Rookie of the Year honors. In only his second season, he won the NBA scoring title.

But David wasn't really happy and fulfilled. Then in 1991 a minister came and helped David understand that "things" - success, possessions, fame, and fortune - cannot satisfy the deepest needs of a person's life. Through a relationship with Jesus Christ, David found a joy and sense of purpose that he had never known.

Many live their entire lives thinking that the things of this world will bring them a lasting joy and satisfaction. But Jesus Christ is the real source of life. Through faith in Him we receive the gift of everlasting life. We also receive the opportunity to experience abundant life here on earth - a life full of meaning and purpose. Jesus said, "I have come that they may have life, and have it to the full" (John 10:10).

Giving as He Gave

See that you also excel in this grace of giving.   II Corinthians 8:7

"I'll never forget this stinking place - or you guys," Chuck Colson promised. "I'll help you somehow." After serving almost seven months in Maxwell Prison, Colson was being released. He had been convicted in 1974 after pleading guilty to obstruction of justice while serving as special counsel to President Richard Nixon.

Now, as a follower of Jesus Christ, the promise he had made to the other prisoners echoed in his mind as he considered his freedom and future. Colson then made the decision to pass up several profitable business opportunities. (One Dallas company had offered him a million dollars in just five years.)

With the help of Christian friends he founded Prison Fellowship, a ministry dedicated to taking the good news of Jesus Christ to prisoners, discipling them, and training them to live honest and productive lives outside of prison. The organization also reaches out to meet the needs of prisoners' families and puts together a gift giving program to children of prisoners during the Christmas season. By 1991, the ministry of Prison Fellowship had spread to 48 states and 40 countries. When Chuck Colson was awarded the Templeton Prize worth over one million dollars, he donated the entire amount to the ministry of Prison Fellowship.

Jesus sacrificially gave Himself for us. Doesn't it make sense that we should give ourselves to Him and to others? II Corinthians 5:15 states that Jesus "died for all, that those who live should no longer live for themselves but for Him who died for them and was raised again." As we follow the example of Jesus, we should no longer live for our own interests and ignore the needs of others. We should give willingly just as Jesus gave.

Consequences

A man reaps what he sows.   Galatians 6:7

Mickey Mantle's heroic accomplishments in baseball were astounding - 536 home runs, .298 career batting average, seven World Championships, and three MVP awards during his 18 years with the New York Yankees. He hit 54 home runs in 1961, just six shy of the record set by Babe Ruth. Mickey played hard and partied harder.

He was haunted by the fear of an early death. His father had died of Hodgkin's Disease at age 40. His grandfather and two uncles had also been stricken with the disease at an early age. As a result, Mickey lived as if there were no tomorrow. A 40-year battle with alcohol was the result of his self-destructive lifestyle. Mickey later admitted that because of alcohol he never fully lived up to his potential. He finally beat the addiction in 1994 only to be diagnosed with liver cancer in 1995.

Perhaps Mickey's greatest feat of heroism took place shortly afterwards as he battled for his life. Having recently trusted Jesus as his Savior, Mickey Mantle appeared before a mass of reporters and courageously stated in the interview, "Don't be like me. I'm no role model."

The Bible clearly says that each of us reap what we sow. "Sow" and "reap" are agricultural or farming terms. Sow means "to plant" and reap means "to harvest." If you sow (plant) apple seed, you reap (harvest) apples. You don't reap bananas. If you want bananas, you have to sow banana seed. The same law is true in human life. If you sow destructive attitudes and actions in your life, you will reap destruction down the road.

While God is able to forgive us when we confess our sins and turn from them, we often must live with the consequences of that sin. While these consequences are damaging to our own lives, many times they have far-reaching effects and hurt others also.

Right Thinking

Finally, brothers, whatever is true, whatever is noble, whatever is right, whatever is pure, whatever is lovely, whatever is admirable - if anything is excellent or praiseworthy - think about such things.

Philippians 4:8

During military maneuvers, a defective grenade exploded in the hand of Sergeant Karoly Takacs. The terrible accident blew off his right hand. Before the accident, Takacs was one of the greatest pistol shooters in the world and part of the Hungarian team expected to win the gold medal in the 1940 Olympics.

Following his release from the hospital, Takacs made the courageous decision to try shooting with his left hand. He constantly practiced in secret so that no one would know of his hopes to compete again. To everyone's astonishment, Takacs not only entered his country's shooting championships in 1939, he was victorious. Unfortunately because of World War II, the 1940 and 1944 Olympics were canceled. During those years, he faithfully served in the Hungarian army and was even promoted to the rank of captain. He never stopped practicing with his left hand.

Following the war, Takacs went on to shock the world by winning the gold medal in pistol shooting at the 1948 and 1952 Olympic Games. When he returned to his homeland, he was honored by his countrymen for his monumental accomplishments. Captain Takacs celebrated by giving himself three presents - three artificial right hands. One was made especially for skiing, one for swimming, and one for boxing.

To accomplish great things, it is important to have a good attitude. Wrong thinking leads to wrong feeling which leads to wrong doing. Therefore it becomes critical that we not allow negative or sinful thoughts invade our minds and take them captive. No matter how bad things may seem to be, God challenges us to focus on those things which are good and positive.

Strength in the Midst of Suffering

But He said to me, "My grace is sufficient for you, for my power is made perfect in weakness." Therefore I will boast all the more gladly about my weaknesses, so that Christ's power may rest on me. That is why, for Christ's sake, I delight in weaknesses, in insults, in hardships, in persecutions, in difficulties. For when I am weak, then I am strong.   II Corinthians 12:9-10

Tim Hansel and his partner were on their way back from a successful snow-ice-rock climb in the Sierras when it happened. With their base camp in view, they approached a natural snow bridge over a glacier crevasse. Unknown to Tim, snow had balled up in the spikes of his hiking boots and it caused him to slip and tumble head first from the bridge. Falling at about 32 feet per second, he landed on the back of his neck almost five stories below. When he came to, his partner was kneeling beside him. Tim remembers feeling fortunate - fortunate he had not landed on the ice pick wrapped around his wrist - fortunate he had not broken his neck and was paralyzed - fortunate to simply be alive.

Tim was miraculously able to walk away from the accident. But when the shock wore off, blinding pain racked his body. Countless doctors and x-rays would later show that he had fractured vertebrae, crushed discs, and bone fragments in his neck. Tim was also informed that the damage - and the pain - was permanent. But in spite of the unavoidable and constant pain of his climbing mishap in 1974, Tim remains a very active Christian. He is the founder of a life changing wilderness survival school, a popular conference speaker, and the author of several best-selling books.

There is never a shortage of God's grace. God's grace is able to save us from our sins. His grace is also able to help us in our suffering. But not only are we able to endure our suffering, His grace and strength enables us to rise above our suffering and accomplish something positive and good with our lives.

The Real Test Of Love

Dear children, let us not love with words or tongue but in actions and in truth. I John 3:18

As the starting defensive tackle for his high school team in Rossville, Illinois, Daniel Huffman dreamed of playing college football someday for Coach Bobby Bowden and the Florida State Seminoles. That was before the summer of his senior year when he made a decision that would end his football career.

Daniel had been raised by his grandparents following his parent's divorce. His grandmother, Shirley, desperately needed a kidney transplant. Because her doctors felt that it could take over a year to find a suitable donor, there were fears that Shirley might die while waiting. That is when Daniel made his decision to donate one of his kidneys so that his grandmother would live. Giving up a kidney meant that he would never again be able to play any contact sports and would need to shelve his dreams of playing for Coach Bowden.

Shirley received her grandson's kidney and is now healthy. Newspapers, television, and radio carried the story of Daniel's sacrificial gift; and he was scheduled to be honored at a football awards ceremony. Also attending this ceremony was Coach Bobby Bowden, who was also on the program to be honored. Coach Bowden first learned of the story while at the ceremony and decided to give him a full scholarship to Florida State to be a student trainer with the football team. Not long afterwards, filming began on a movie to be televised on the Showtime cable network: *A Gift of Love: The Daniel Huffman Story.*

The real test of love is not in what we say but in what we do. In the Christian life, there is a priority placed on loving God and others. But anyone can say "I love you." Real love is demonstrated in "actions and in truth." God proved his great love for us because even "while we were still sinners, Christ died for us" (Romans 5:8).

Only Trust Him

Trust in the LORD with all your heart and lean not on your own understanding.   Proverbs 3:5-6

It was September 2, 1814, when Francis Scott Key set sail on the Minden. He had been sent by President Madison to negotiate for the release of an American doctor who was being held illegally on board a British warship. What Key and the Americans did not know as they approached the British vessel was that the British were readying themselves to attack Fort McHenry in Baltimore.

When Key spoke to the British officers they informed him of their plan to attack the American fort. Because they could not afford to allow Key to return and warn them of the upcoming attack, he and the other Americans were rounded up at gunpoint and taken aboard the British warship. Shortly afterwards, Key helplessly watched as the British warship began its attack on the American fort. Throughout the night the cannons boomed and the rockets blazed through the skies as the British fired upon Fort McHenry.

As he paced the deck, Key prayed that the American army would be able to hold its position. He hoped that in the morning he would not see a flag of surrrender flying above the fort. When the sun finally came up, Key looked toward Fort McHenry and saw the stars and stripes of the American flag still waving. He then took out a pencil and paper and expressed his feelings of joy and thanksgiving. The result was a beautiful and inspiring poem that was later set to music, "The Star Spangled Banner." The fouth stanza of the National Anthem contains the words, "This be our motto, in God is our trust." These words, "In God We Trust," have since become our motto as a nation.

Our trust as a nation should never be in our military strength, nor our wealth, nor our celebrated past. Our trust as a nation and as individuals should be in the eternal God of the universe. "In God We Trust." May we never forget our Christian heritage.

Our Symbol of Hope

Christ in you, the hope of glory.   Colossians 1:27

When Helen Keller was only 20 months old, she suffered a high fever that mystified her doctors. When the fever finally broke, little Helen was left completely blind and deaf. Because she was cut off from much of the world around her, she soon forgot how to talk. Helen would often kick and scream for hours because she was frustrated and unable to communicate. While others believed she was mentally ill and should be institutionalized, Helen's parents would not give up hope.

Three months before Helen's 7th birthday, Annie Sullivan came to be her teacher. It took her three difficult weeks just to break Helen from her disobedience and tantrums. Soon afterwards, she learned to communicate as Miss Sullivan repeatedly spelled out words on Helen's palm. Despite her handicaps, Helen made remarkable progress. She learned to read Braille. She learned to write. She learned to "hear" by placing her fingers on the lips of the person talking. She even learned to speak by imitating the position of their lips and tongue. In 1900, Helen entered Radcliffe College at the age of 20. In 1904, she graduated with honors.

During her adult life Helen Keller authored books, visited hospitals to encourage wounded soldiers during World War II, lectured around the world, and helped raise money for the American Foundation for the Blind. In 1964, she was awarded the Medal of Freedom, which is America's highest civilian award. Because of her courage and accomplishment in spite of her disability, Helen Keller became a symbol of hope all over the world.

For every Christian, **our symbol of hope** is Jesus Christ. Because of His sacrificial death on the cross we can be forgiven of our sins. Because he overcame death and now lives we too shall live. Jesus said, "I am the way and the truth and the life" (John 14:6). Our symbol of hope in this life and the life to come is Jesus Christ.

Follow The Leader

Follow my example, as I follow the example of Christ.

I Corinthians 11:1

Terry Fox was a very active and athletic teenager when he was diagnosed with bone cancer, and doctors were forced to amputate his right leg above the knee. While in the cancer ward of the hospital he became acutely aware of the suffering of cancer patients. Moved by their suffering and inspired by an article he had read about an amputee completing the New York Marathon, Terry decided to run across Canada. His hope was to raise money and awareness for cancer research.

Fitted with an artificial leg he diligently trained for 15 months and began his "Marathon of Hope" in April, 1980. Through rain, snow, hail and extreme heat, Terry ran for 143 days, averaging approximately 26 miles per day. People all over the world were shocked and saddened when Terry was forced to quit his "Marathon of Hope" on September 1 after cancer was found in his lungs. He died of cancer 10 months later at the age of 22.

Over $270 million has been raised in Terry's name to fund cancer research. Inspired by Terry Fox's story, Canadian Steve Fonyo completed the 4,924 mile run across Canada in 1985. Like Terry Fox, he had lost a leg to cancer.

Paul writes to the Corinthians, "Follow my example, as I follow the example of Christ." He also wrote to the Philippians, "Whatever you have learned or received or heard from me, or seen in me--put it into practice" (4:9). Our pattern for living should be Jesus Christ. As we follow Him, our lives should inspire and empower others to also follow Jesus Christ.

Tests and Trials

Consider it pure joy, my brothers, whenever you face trials of many kinds, because you know that the testing of your faith develops perseverance.   James 1:2-3

It was a miracle that French soldier Joseph Guillemot was still alive. While in combat against the Germans during World War I, his lungs were severely burned by a poisonous gas attack. Once the doctors knew that he would survive, they were unsure how to treat his terribly scarred lungs. Believing that deep breathing would benefit the healing process, doctors prescribed a program of long distance running.

As a result, Joseph not only returned to active duty as a soldier, he also began running in races when the war was finally over. A physical exam showed that his scarred lungs were no longer a problem. After several victories, Joseph Guillemot was selected to represent France at the 1920 Olympics.

On August 17, the 20-year-old "miracle soldier" lined up against 16 of the world's fastest runners in the 5,000 meters. The competition included Paavo Nurmi, who is remembered as the greatest distance runner in history. Joseph followed Paavo throughout the race and eventually passed the legendary runner to win by 15 meters.

Would Joseph Guillemot have been an Olympic champion if it had not been for the burns he received during World War I? Probably not. His abilities as a runner were developed as a result of the program of running that his doctors prescribed to bring about the healing of his scarred lungs.

Sometimes it is hard to find anything good in the testing and trials of life. But tests and trials benefit us because they both prove us and improve us. For example, a math test demonstrates or proves knowledge and abilities in the subject. It also improves math skills as I am forced to study, prepare, and take the test. In the life of the

Christian, God uses tests and trials to prove the quality of our faith and character, and also to push us beyond our comfort zone and spur us on to become more like Christ.

Forgetting Yourself

Do nothing out of selfish ambition or vain conceit, but in humility consider others better than yourselves. Each of you should look not only to your own interests, but also to the interests of others.

Philippians 2:3-4

The Battle of Gettysburg took place during the first three days of July in 1863. General George Meade's Northern army of 85,000 waged a bloody battle against General Robert E. Lee's Southern army of 65,000. Gettysburg would become a turning point in the Civil War. Because of casualties to the Southern army, which numbered nearly 23,000 men, General Lee was never again able to launch a major offensive against the North.

During the third day of battle, it seems that General Alexander S. Webb forgot his high position as commander of the Second Brigade and spent the entire day on the firing line. When he noticed a company of Rebels clearing a stone wall to attack a Northern regiment, Webb raced down the line to warn them. He then directed the attack against the Rebels. A fierce battle followed in which General Webb was shot, and more than half of his men were killed or wounded. But inspired by the heroic bravery of its General, the regiment courageously stood its ground. Afterwards, General Alexander Webb received a Medal of Honor for an act which General Meade stated surpassed that of any other General in the field of battle at Gettysburg.

God places a great value on humility. In fact, James 4:6 states that "God opposes the proud but gives grace to the humble." Humility is a proper estimate of our self in relation to God our creator and sustainer. It is also a proper estimate of our self in relation to others. A truly humble person does not think "too highly" of himself but is submissive to God and considerate of the needs of others.

Following the Crowd

Do not conform any longer to the pattern of this world.

Romans 12:2

Ken Davis, a famous Christian comedian and writer, met Debbie after speaking at a high school assembly. She was crippled and her face badly scarred from an apparent accident. Debbie shared her story with Ken as tears streamed down her once beautiful face. After a football game she and some friends went out on a deserted road and began drinking alcohol. Even though she wasn't a "party animal," Debbie went along with her friends.

After they had gotten drunk they began playing a game called "chicken." The game is played by two cars driving toward each other at a fast speed. The first car to turn out of the path of the other oncoming car loses the game and is the "chicken."

Debbie wasn't comfortable being at the party in the first place, and now she was terrified as the game of "chicken" began. She wanted to ask her friends to take her home or at least let her out of the car, but she was afraid of what her friends would think of her. The cars barely missed each other twice, and Debbie feared for her life, but she remained silent - afraid of losing her friends.

During the third and final game, no one pulled away and both cars collided head-on. All of Debbie's friends were killed. Only she survived. Debbie's crippled body and disfigured face are a daily reminder of the power of peer pressure and her foolish decision to remain silent on that fateful night.

The need for friendship, acceptance, and popularity makes peer pressure a powerful force - especially in the lives of children and teens. But sometimes the pressure to "fit in" or "follow the crowd" can be harmful and even dangerous.

God instructs us, "Do not conform any longer to the pattern of this world." That means that we shouldn't allow others to shape our lives and make our decisions for us. When we are faced with peer pressure and feel the need to "fit in" and "follow the crowd," we need wisely and bravely to stand for what we believe is right. The decision we make could mean the difference between life and death.

Feeling Special!

For you created my inmost being; you knit me together in my mother's womb. I praise you because I am fearfully and wonderfully made.   Psalm 139:13-14

As Ripley would say, "Believe it or not":

- The human heart pumps about 72 times each minute, or 40 million times a year.

- Even though the heart is only about the size of a fist, it will pump about 450,000 tons of blood in a lifetime.

- An adult human has about 75,000 miles of blood vessels which pump about 450 tons of blood during a lifetime.

- Despite being no thicker than 3/16 of an inch, human skin helps control body temperature and is nearly waterproof.

- Each human being begins with only one cell which multiplies and grows to over 26 billion cells.

- The human eye, which is about the size of a ping pong ball, can handle about 1 1/2 million messages at one time.

- The human brain weighs only 2 to 3 pounds and is made up of 30 billion cells yet never gets tired.

- The human nervous system works like telephone wires and is capable of carrying messages at 300 miles per hour.

Each of us is a living miracle, skillfully crafted by a God who loves us more than we can imagine. Feeling special yet? You should!

The Grip Of Sin

Let us throw off everything that hinders and the sin that so easily entangles.   Hebrews 12:1

While on a field trip, Morris and a couple of buddies went off on their own to explore Wild Cat Cave. His two friends left after a few minutes and took the flashlight with them. Though the cave was dark, Morris stayed behind to examine a narrow passage that was only 15 inches wide. He squeezed his slender body through the opening and inched his way along the dark passage. Suddenly Morris slipped and fell. The next thing he knew he was trapped in a narrow crack with his right arm pinned beneath him. He desperately scratched and pulled at the cave wall with his free hand but could not free himself.

Shortly afterwards, Morris' teacher noticed that he was missing and began a search. When their search brought them back to Wild Cat Cave, they found Morris yelling for help. Firemen were called to the scene but were unable to squeeze into the passage and get close enough to pull him to freedom.

Several hours passed and a large crowd, including the news media, gathered at the mouth of the cave. Even experienced rescue teams were unable to come up with a plan that would get them close enough to free him. After several hours and several failed attempts to rescue him, Morris lost hope that he would ever be free and began to cry.

Finally, after being trapped for over 26 hours, Morris was freed when 15-year-old Michael Ulrich managed to squeeze his way through the dark passage. He then tied several straps and ropes to Morris, allowing the rescuers to pull him to freedom.

Sin "easily entangles" and traps us. Its powerful grip holds us in spiritual bondage, and we are unable to free ourselves. But Jesus is able to do what we cannot do on our own. He came to set the captive free from the penalty and power of sin.

One Step

For it is by grace you have been saved, through faith.

Ephesians 2:8

Billions of people from around the world sat glued to their television sets on July 20, 1969. They breathlessly watched as over a half a million miles from earth, the space module named "Eagle" descended to the moon's surface. This historic day was the result of 10 years of effort by America's space program and cost billions of dollars. Over 400,000 people in assembly plants and control rooms had worked to make this day possible.

Inside the Eagle were astronauts Neil Armstrong and "Buzz" Aldrin. Moments later, TV viewers heard Armstrong say, "The Eagle has landed!" He then climbed down the ladder and became the first man to walk on the moon. A quiet and modest Neil Armstrong spoke the now famous words to the billions who listened in, "That's one small step for man and one giant leap for mankind!"

Almost 2,000 years ago, Jesus took our place and died on a cross for our sins. He paid the debt or penalty that we could not pay. By doing so, Jesus has prepared the way for each of us to take a very, very important step. That step is - faith in Him. By placing our faith in Jesus we receive the forgiveness of sin and eternal life. That one step is the most important step that any human being can take. That one step literally makes all the difference in the world.

Bad Company

Do not be misled: "Bad company corrupts good character."
I Corinthians 15:33

Len Bias was the No. 2 college player taken in the 1986 NBA draft. Taken by the Boston Celtics, he was expected to be the type of player that would help the team win another championship. His coach at the University of Maryland called Len Bias "the greatest basketball player that ever played in the Atlantic Coast Conference." He was 6-9 and weighed 220 - but was described as cat-quick with the ability to handle the ball, dribble, and shoot. He had averaged 23 points a game while earning "Player of the Year" honors in the Atlantic Coast Conference and was being compared to Michael Jordan.

Just two days after the draft Len Bias collapsed in his dorm room and died. Some "so-called" friends had come by to celebrate with him after the draft. They brought with them some crack cocaine. He tried the drug and it cost him his life.

Len Bias allowed himself to be in the company of a wrong crowd involved in a wrong activity. As a result, he never played one game with the Boston Celtics, nor did he enjoy one dime of his million dollar contract. But worse than that - a foolish decision to go along with the crowd and do drugs cost him his life.

Two important lessons can be learned from this tragedy: Number 1: We need to be very careful of the company we keep because "Bad company corrupts good character." Number 2: "We reap what we sow" - meaning that foolish and wrong decisions result in consequences.

The Truth and Nothing but the Truth

Then you will know the truth, and the truth will set you free.

John 8:32

Rubin "Hurricane" Carter was the No. 1 middleweight boxing contender in the world when he was wrongfully imprisoned and sentenced to a triple life sentence. His trial had been built on false evidence, cheating, lies, suppressing evidence and witness tampering. When the trial ended, an all-white jury found the black boxer guilty of killing three whites at the Lafayette Grill in New Jersey. Throughout the proceedings Carter proclaimed his innocence.

Prison life separated him from his wife and two children, and he eventually divorced his wife to lessen her pain. Carter also lost the sight in one eye due to a botched operation performed during his prison stay. He once spent an entire month in solitary confinement, and when he was finally released his clothes had literally rotted off of his body.

During his imprisonment Carter wrote a book pleading for help in his fight for justice and freedom entitled, *The Seventh Round.* After reading the book an unlikely group of Canadians, along with a black teenager from the Bronx, believed that Carter had been terribly wronged. They moved close to the prison in New Jersey and committed themselves to study every detail of the case and help his lawyers. The truth they discovered resulted in a new trial. Rubin "Hurricane" Carter was set free in 1988 after 21 years of imprisonment.

Just as Rubin "Hurricane" Carter was set free by the truth, the truth of God's Word has the power to free anyone from the slavery of sin. Through the reading and obedience of His words of truth, we are set free from the power and penalty of sin.

The Reward of Perseverance

Endure hardship with us like a good soldier of Christ Jesus.

II Timothy 2:3

Paul Wittgenstein gave his first big piano concert at the age of 26, and critics applauded his exceptional talent. But when World War I began shortly afterwards he put his career on hold and enlisted in the Austrian army. While fighting on the Russian front lines Paul was hit by a bullet that shattered his right arm. He was then taken prisoner of war. To save his life doctors at the prison hospital were forced to remove his arm.

When he regained consciousness Paul thought all his dreams and plans to be a great pianist had come to an end. But his discouragement turned to hope as he bravely committed himself to play again someday. He was eventually released as a prisoner and went home.

Finally able to begin practicing the piano, he was faced with two problems: how to make his one remaining hand play the keys in such a way as to sound like he were playing with two, and there was very little serious music written for a one-handed pianist.

After months of arranging music for his left hand and practicing seven hours a day, Paul Wittgenstein gave his first concert using only his left hand. Music critics wholeheartedly agreed that he was truly a gifted musician.

Every good soldier must persevere and endure hardships. Being a Christian means being a soldier in the army of the Lord. As we experience hardships and setbacks it is so very important to persevere and continue doing His work and accomplishing His mission here on earth. God's Word promises every Christian that He will always reward our perseverance and good works.

Like Us

And being found in appearance as a man, He humbled himself.

Philippians 2:8

During the 1950's, a very unique book was written that was entitled *Black Like Me*. The author, John Howard Griffin, was white. Feeling that he could never really understand the prejudices, discrimination, and injustices that a black man experienced in the South, he made himself black. Griffin shaved the straight hair from his head and darkened his pale skin with the use of medication, sun lamp treatments and stains.

Posing as a black man, he then traveled throughout the South. His whole world changed. There were hotels in which he was not allowed to stay. There were restaurants in which he was not allowed to eat. There were restrooms and water fountains he was not allowed to use. There were vehicles in which he was not allowed to ride. Day-to-day, Griffin was denied certain opportunities and privileges. Much of the treatment he received was inhuman. He recorded his experiences in the book *Black Like Me*.

The Bible tells us that Jesus clothed Himself in flesh and bone, became a man and lived on this earth for nearly 33 years. Because He left the splendor of heaven and dwelled among us he is able to understand us. He celebrates with us in our victories, successes, joys, and laughter. He also sympathizes with us in pain, suffering, temptations, and losses. This knowledge should be a great strength and comfort to us as we live our lives.

No Room

She wrapped Him in cloths and placed Him in a manger, because there was no room for them in the inn. Luke 2:7

During the fall of 1775 the manager of the largest hotel in Baltimore refused to give a room to a man who was dressed as a farmer. He felt that the man's lowly appearance would discredit his fine hotel. Refused a place to sleep for the night, the man went elsewhere.

Later the manager discovered that the man he had turned away was none other than Thomas Jefferson, who at that time was Vice President of the United States. He immediately sent a message to Jefferson inviting him back to the hotel as his special guest. Jefferson had this message taken back to the manager: "Tell him I have already engaged a room. I value his good intentions highly, but if he has no place for a dirty American farmer, he has none for the Vice President of the United States."

Jesus Christ, the King of Kings and Lord of Lords, left His throne in heaven and became the baby of a lowly peasant girl. On the night of His birth there was no room for Him in the inn. He spent His first night on earth in a feeding trough, wrapped in the cloths used to wipe down the animals, in the company of farm animals. Jesus Christ did all of this with each of us in mind. In our busy and active lives there is an important question that we each need to ask ourselves: Do we have room for the King of Kings and Lord of Lords - in our hearts and in our lives?

Too Heavy A Load

Come to me, all you who are weary and burdened, and I will give you rest.   Matthew 11:28

The Flying Wallendas were considered by many as the greatest tightrope walkers in the history of circus. They were the exciting climax of the Ringling Brothers Barnum and Bailey Circus. One of their death-defying feats included a four level pyramid of four or five on the bottom and a little girl at the top. Maintaining this pyramid, they would walk across the tightrope from one side of the circus arena to the other. Incredibly, the Flying Wallendas accomplished this feat night after night all over the world.

During one performance in Detroit they built their famous four level pyramid and walked the tightrope just as they had successfully done many times before. But about two-thirds of the way across, one of the men at the bottom of the pyramid began to tremble and cried out that he could no longer hold the upper levels. The entire pyramid crashed to the circus floor. The tragedy crippled several of the Wallendas, and one of the members was killed.

There are times when each of us feels like the pressures of life are more than we can handle. We may feel like we're trying to balance on a tightrope. We're tired and trembling, and to make matters worse we are carrying a heavy burden that is too much to bear. What do we do?

Don't Give Up! Jesus said, "Come to me, all you who are weary and burdened, and I will give you rest." We may be unable to handle our problems - but Jesus is more than able. Peter advises us in his first letter, chapter 5 verse 7: "Cast all your anxiety on Him because He cares for you."

Remember!

This is my body given for you; do this in remembrance of me.

Luke 22:19

On the frigid morning of December 14, 2000, Robert Lee Robinson and Chris Grays were working on the deck of a barge on the Mississippi River. Due to an ice storm earlier in the week ice still covered the barge. It also covered the crane and cable used to unload the cargo at the Port of West Memphis.

Without any warning the crane began collapsing. Robinson heard it, Grays did not. Robinson could have stepped safely out of the way of the 75-foot steel boom. Instead, he quickly stepped in and shoved Chris Grays causing him to stumble out of the way. The boom glanced off of Grays' stomach, knocking him to his hands and knees. When he looked back, he saw Robinson pinned beneath the heavy boom. His friend and savior looked up at him for a moment and then died.

Since the accident Grays has spent many a sleepless night. He can't help but remember how his best friend gave his life for him.

"This is my body given for you; do this in remembrance of me." Jesus spoke these words during the Last Supper with His disciples before His death. Jesus calls for us to remember Him and the life that He gave and the death that He died. While we were sinners, Jesus suffered in our place and died for us so that through belief in Him we might have forgiveness and everlasting life. REMEMBER!

Contentment Within

I have learned the secret of being content in any and every situation.
                                                            Philippians 4:12

It was a freak accident. During a game against Ohio State in the fall of 2000, 19-year old Adam Taliaferro of Penn State severely injured his spine. He was making a head first tackle against a 231-pound running back when his head snapped back and nearly severed his spinal chord. Doctors successfully performed a spinal fusion, and Adam was then transferred to another out-of-state hospital to begin the long and torturous road to recovery. Doctors and therapists pushed him daily through workouts that lasted up to five hours.

Almost 3 1/2 months after the injury, Adam Taliaferro left the hospital on crutches. Even though he will never be able to suit up and play another game of football, Adam was thankful he was going home and would someday walk normally again.

Contentment is an attitude of thanksgiving and satisfaction on the inside no matter how things may be on the outside. Paul wrote: "I have learned the secret of being content in any and every situation." It is interesting to know that Paul wrote these words while in a Roman prison waiting to die. The "secret of being content" that Paul mentions in this verse - is a personal knowledge of Jesus Christ and His ability to supply our needs even when times are difficult.

Passion to Pray

And being in anguish, He prayed more earnestly, and His sweat was like drops of blood falling to the ground.   Luke 22:44

The fall of Philadelphia during the Revolutionary War was a massive blow to the Americans' fight for freedom. Because they were not strong enough to stop the British, George Washington led his army just 15 miles away to set up camp for the winter.

While the enemy enjoyed the comforts of home in Philadelphia, Washington and his men had little protection against the cruel winter months. They built shelters from anything available; logs, fence rails, mud and straw. But it seemed impossible to stay warm. They didn't have adequate clothing for the freezing weather and snow. Some of the men had no shirts or shoes, and there were few blankets. Wind and rain drifted through the windows and cracks of the huts, and rain dripped through the roof. Food was also in short supply and often consisted of nothing more than firecakes (cornmeal mixed with water).

During those harsh months of hunger, sickness and despair, George Washington sought the help and guidance of God Almighty. A farmer once found the great General all alone outside of the camp. He was on his knees in the snow, his cheeks wet with tears as he prayed. Washington believed that God would deliver them in some way. When spring finally came those who survived marched with renewed hope to fight the British and win their freedom.

We are told in Luke 22:44 that Jesus Christ prayed on the night before His suffering and death. If Jesus, the Son of God, found a need to pray in this difficult hour, how much more should you and I pray during difficult times? Prayer is an awesome privilege. It allows us to enter the very presence of an almighty God who loves us and desires the very best for us. God's Word instructs us to "pray continually." But during times of difficulty, our prayers need to take on a greater energy and passion like the Lord Jesus.

Ambassadors of the King

We are therefore Christ's ambassadors.   II Corinthians 5:20

They had no mother or father, no home, no one to love or care for them and no one to teach them the difference between right and wrong. As a result, the orphaned boys of Omaha, Nebraska roamed the streets looking for trouble. Father Flanagan saw the problem and recognized the need for the boys to have a loving home in which to grow up.

So, in 1921 he borrowed money and rented an old house. He then went door to door asking for anything his neighbors could spare in order to furnish the house. While some thought he was foolish, Father Flanagan persevered and opened his home for orphaned and homeless boys. Beginning with just five boys it wasn't long before more and more came, and they eventually outgrew the house.

Believing the boys needed more space, Father Flanagan bought a nearby farm and built Boys Town. With the help of friends and neighbors they built houses, shops, a pool, a post office, a school, a church, and a large dining hall where all the boys could eat together. Homeless and orphaned boys from all over the country came to live at Boys Town.

Ambassador is defined as a representative of a royal court. As a Christian we are an ambassador, or representative, of the King of Kings - Jesus Christ. While He lived on earth and "dwelt among us", Jesus Christ ministered to the needy. We are now His ambassadors, and our duty is to carry on the work that He began nearly 2,000 years ago. Each day our prayer should be that God would open our eyes to see the needs around us and then strengthen us to do His will.

A Clear Conscience

So I strive always to keep my conscience clear before God and man.
Acts 24:16

How honest was "Honest" Abe? It seems that as a young man, Abraham Lincoln worked as a clerk in a general store. On one particular day he added up the purchase of a woman and charged her two dollars and six cents. Later that evening he closed the store and counted the earnings for the day. It was then that Abe noticed he had six cents too much and realized he had overcharged the woman.

Even though six cents was very little money, Abe believed that his wrong must be made right. So he set out on foot for the woman's home nearly three miles outside of town. Through the darkness he hiked through fields and forest until he arrived at the customer's home where he explained the mistake and returned the six cents.

This kind of honesty became a distinguishing characteristic of the man who would become the 16th President of the United States. Holding firmly to his convictions, Abraham Lincoln became one of history's greatest leaders and led the nation in abolishing slavery.

Jesus clearly informs us in Matthew 7 that we will be known by our actions. Others will identify us and label us based on our character - or lack of it. Therefore, we ought to go to great lengths to live honestly and keep our "conscience clear before God and man."

Keeping the Faith

As I was with Moses, so I will be with you; I will never leave you nor forsake you.   Joshua 1:5

As the "Father" of the Protestant Reformation, Martin Luther is recognized as one of the most influential figures in the history of Christianity and the world. His translation of the Bible and other writings have helped millions understand the fundamentals of the Christian life. He also played an important role in the history of music, writing such great hymns as "A Mighty Fortress Is Our God."

Katherine was his wife of many years. Once during their marriage Martin was deeply discouraged and depressed. He could barely eat or sleep for several weeks and was unable to get any work done on his translation of the Bible. Worried about her husband, Katherine came up with an interesting plan. Dressing herself in black "mourning" clothes and a veil, she entered his place of study.

When Martin saw her he was shocked and asked who had died. She cried and responded, "Oh, it is terrible! God is dead." He then responded, "God is dead? What in heaven's name are you talking about?" Katherine simply replied, "Well, judging from the way you have been acting the past few weeks, God must be dead. If He weren't, you would use your great faith in Him to help you out of this depression and inactivity." Struck by her words, Martin took her in his arms and whispered, "You are right. Now go change those clothes and I will get busy."

The Christian life is a life of faith, trusting God to be present with us at all times, never leaving or abandoning us. You may remember that when Jesus came to earth, He was given the name Emmanuel, meaning "God with us." He is the God who is near. Therefore, even in life's most discouraging and troubling moments, the Christian has reason to take hope. SO KEEP THE FAITH!

Working Hard or Hardly Working

Well done, good and faithful servant! You have been faithful with a few things; I will put you in charge of many things. Come and share your master's happiness!   Matthew 25:23

The ancient people of Greece used imagined or fictional stories called "myths" to answer the questions they had about life and the world around them. One of the greatest and most celebrated heroes of Greek mythology was Hercules. He was a man of great strength and courage and performed 12 extraordinary tasks.

According to one story, a common laborer was driving a team of horses that was pulling a wagon loaded with supplies. Because of the heavy load the wheels sank so deep into the mud that the horses were unable to move the wagon. Feeling helpless, the man began to cry and call out for Hercules. The legendary Hercules finally appeared and found the man sitting by the road in self-pity and despair. He said to the man, "Put your shoulder to the wheel, man, and drive the horses. Then you may call on the great Hercules to help you. If you won't lift a finger to help yourself, why would you expect Hercules or anyone else to assist you."

Jesus' parable in Matthew 25 condemns the servant who is foolish, lazy and undisciplined - and rewards the productive and faithful servant. We are to be wise and hard workers in this life - in our daily duties and responsibilities - and especially in our service to the Lord.

How Big Is God?

For nothing is impossible with God.   Luke 1:37

Tommy John was the leading pitcher in the National League during the 1974 baseball season, and it looked as if he would lead his team to the World Series. But it wasn't to be. Late in the season he ruptured a ligament in his pitching elbow. Doctors said that his chances of pitching again were perhaps "one in a hundred."

Not long after the operation he and his family attended church. When the preacher finally stepped to the pulpit he delivered a sermon on Abraham and Sarah. Though this elderly couple had lost all hope of having any children of their own, God promised them a son. Abraham was 100 years old, and Sarah was in her 70's when she became pregnant and gave birth to Isaac. Tommy John remembers the minister looking straight at him and saying, "You know, with God, nothing is impossible."

Encouraged by the minister's words, Tommy began his comeback. When the cast finally came off he began a daily routine of grueling workouts that lasted nearly 18 months. He did make it back to the Major Leagues. In fact, Tommy John pitched more games after the injury than he had before and eventually pitched in the World Series.

I read somewhere once that "our God is too small." The author really didn't mean that our God is small but that our view of God is too small, and, as a result our faith in God is also small. In this life that we live we often allow hardships to discourage us and steal away our hope. One thing you can count on is hardship. It is a part of living. Therefore, we need to trust in a God who is unlimited in power and ability. Remember, "nothing is impossible with God."

Keeping Our Goals Before Us

I press on toward the goal to win the prize for which God has called me heavenward in Christ Jesus.   Philippians 3:14

She had been the first woman to swim successfully the English Channel in both directions. Florence Chadwick's new goal was to swim the waters that separated Catalina Island from the California coast. When she entered the waters in 1952 the conditions were less than ideal. Not only was the water extremely cold, but a thick fog made it difficult for the boat that accompanied her to see her as she swam. This made the swim especially dangerous because their job was to keep any sharks safely at a distance.

Several times during her swim Florence heard gunshots as the boat chased off sharks. She bravely struggled for more than 15 hours - but finally asked to be pulled aboard the boat. Her coach tried to convince her that land was near and encouraged her to continue, but she was unable to see anything above the waters and through the fog. Florence Chadwick quit - only a half mile from her final goal. She later admitted that if she could have just seen the land - she would have made it.

Somebody wisely said, "Aim at nothing. And that is exactly what you will hit. Nothing!" In every endeavor in life we need goals. We need something at which to aim our efforts and energies. As followers of Christ our primary goal should be to know Him better and become more and more like Him in our attitudes, actions and words. In all of life's endeavors - but especially in our Christian duties - "press on toward the goal."

The "Real" Winner

Do not let anyone look down on you because you are young, but set an example for the believers in speech, in life, in love, in faith and in purity.   I Timothy 4:12

Boys and girls from all over the country nervously took their places on the stage for the National Spelling Bee held in Washington. During the fourth round of the contest 11-year-old Rosalie Elliot stepped to center stage and was asked to spell the word "avowal". Because of her soft voice and southern accent, the judges were unsure of her spelling. For several minutes they debated as they replayed recordings of her spelling the word.

While all of this was going on, Rosalie overheard the other contestants behind her as they whispered the correct spelling. When she did she realized she had misspelled the word. Finally the judges, unable to come to a unanimous decision on Rosalie's spelling, decided to ask her to repeat her original spelling of the word "avowal." Without hesitating, Rosalie honestly admitted that she had misspelled the word and quietly stepped off the stage.

As she left, the audience responded with a standing ovation. Along with them stood almost 50 reporters who had come to cover the event. The really big story the following day, and in the years to come, was not of the Spelling Bee Champ, but of the little girl who won their respect with her honesty.

Youthfulness is no excuse for a lifestyle of sin and dishonesty. Even the young are encouraged to live their lives in such a way as to set an example for others. In Matthew 5:16, Jesus stated, "Let your light shine before men, that they may see your good deeds and praise your Father in heaven."

Knowing Your Part

I have hidden your word in my heart that I might not sin against you.   Psalm 119:11

When he was in his 80's, actor George Burns was what he called "semi-retired" and had not acted in a movie in nearly 35 years. But then his agent suggested that he play the leading role along with Walter Matthau in the movie, "The Sunshine Boys." The producer and director hired Burns but were a little skeptical because of his age. They thought he might have trouble remembering his lines and slow production.

A cast rehearsal was called shortly before filming began. The producer and director became even more concerned about their decision to hire Burns when he showed up without his manuscript. They assumed that his memory had failed. But, to their amazement, Burns had already memorized his lines and the lines of every other cast member. His part in the movie earned George Burns an Academy Award.

An actor is expected to know his part. In order to do so he must spend much time and effort memorizing lines. How much more should we as Christians study and know God's Word?

Psalm 119 instructs us to hide God's Word in our hearts. Joshua 1:8 instructs us to "meditate on it day and night." You and I should study to know God's Word - not for an earthly trophy like an Academy Award - but to know God and His direction for our lives and to receive an eternal reward in heaven.

Free To Set Others Free

Freely you have received, freely give.   Matthew 10:8

Harriet Tubman was born into slavery nearly 40 years before the Civil War. At the age of 24 she married a free Negro man named John and later shared with him her hope of someday running away. She had heard of the Underground Railroad - a network of stations or stops that secretly helped slaves travel to free states in the north. Though her husband told her that he would inform her master if she tried to escape, Harriet silently longed for freedom and slipped away one night in 1849 - without her husband.

She traveled only at night and often through the woods to avoid capture. During her escape Harriet once traveled in a wagon under a load of vegetables. On another occasion she stayed for a week in the potato hole of a cabin that belonged to a free black family. She finally arrived in the free state of Pennsylvania after traveling nearly 90 miles.

No longer in danger, Harriet did not simply "kick-back," retire and enjoy a life of freedom and ease. She vowed to help others gain their freedom. During the 1850's she made 19 rescue trips and helped free 300 slaves. Even though a $40,000 reward was offered for her capture she was never caught and never lost a slave. In 1857 Harriet Tubman led her own parents to freedom.

The believer has been freely given forgiveness and eternal life through the sacrificial death of the Jesus Christ. As a result we are set free from the power and the penalty of sin and death. It is now our privilege and duty to lead others to freedom by living a life of service to Christ - sharing his message of Good News - with our words and our lives.

Power In The Blood

The blood of Jesus, His Son, purifies us from all sin.   I John 1:7

Grieving over the loss of his granddaughter to "black diphtheria," Dr. Felix Ruh vowed to find a cure for the dreaded disease. In his commitment to do so, he spent endless hours locked inside his laboratory with his co-worker, Louis Pasteur. After several months of culturing a container of the disease, twenty beautiful and healthy horses were brought to the laboratory. The mouth, eyes and nose of each of the horses were then exposed to the deadly germ.

Every one of the horses developed an extremely high fever, and nineteen of the twenty horses died. Slowly, the fever of the one remaining horse began to drop, and it eventually recuperated from the disease that had killed so many. The healthy animal was then killed and the blood drawn from its veins. Without delay, the blood was taken to a hospital in Paris, where nearly 300 babies were dying from the disease. The blood of the horse that had overcome the dreaded disease was then injected into the dying babies. All but three of those babies completely recovered.

The Bible is clear in stating that "all have sinned" (Romans 3:23) and our sin justly deserves punishment, "for the wages of sin is death" (Romans 6:23). But Jesus Christ shed His own innocent blood as a sacrifice for you and for me. He then miraculously overcame sin and death by rising from the grave and ascending into heaven. As a result, the blood of Jesus Christ has the power to cleanse us from all sin and heal our soul's diseases. "For God so loved the world that He gave His one and only Son, that whoever believes in Him shall not perish but have eternal life" (John 3:16).

"A Mind Is A Terrible Thing To Waste"

Since, then, you have been raised with Christ, set your hearts on things above, where Christ is seated at the right hand of God. Set your minds on things above, not on earthly things.

Colossians 3:1-2

Captured and imprisoned during the war with North Vietnam, Major James Nesmeth spent seven years in a tiny cage that was only 4 1/2 feet high and 5 feet long. He was all alone and had little physical activity to occupy his day. Under these trying circumstances, Nesmeth was afraid of losing his sanity. He decided he needed to find something enjoyable to occupy his mind. Since he loved golf he began to imagine playing 18 holes each day. Approximately four hours a day Nesmeth carefully visualized every detail of the game - the drive, the chip shot and the putt.

When Major Nesmeth was finally released and stepped onto a golf course, he had not even touched a club in the last seven years. Before the war he had been a weekend golfer with an average in the 90's. But on that day, when he finished 18 holes, Nesmeth had scored an amazing 74, nearly 20 stokes better than before. His only practice for the last seven years had been ... in his mind.

After many years of study, even the greatest scientists still don't fully understand the capabilities and potential of the human brain. But God does. He designed and created this awesome part of our body and fully understands its capabilities. Because of the power of our minds to influence the way we live, God instructs the Christian to take our focus off the things of the world and its pleasures - and set our desires and thoughts on "things above."

A 24-Hour Gift

Do not boast about tomorrow, for you do not know what a day may bring forth.   Proverbs 27:1

Following a game against the University of Colorado, the Oklahoma State basketball team boarded two jets and a twin-engine plane on January 27, 2001, to return home. At takeoff the temperature was minus 4 degrees with light snow and visibility of approximately one mile. Though the crews had been warned that ice could form on the wings, conditions were not harsh enough for airport authorities to ground the aircraft.

Witnesses saw the twin-engine plane takeoff, level off at 23,000 feet, bank hard to the right and suddenly go straight down. It crashed in a field 40 miles east of Denver killing 10 people, eight of whom were associated with the O.S.U basketball program, including players Nate Fleming and Daniel Lawson.

Coach Eddie Sutton spoke to reporters three days after the crash saying, "I told our team that life is so precious and sometimes we take it for granted. One thing they must understand is they better live every day like it might be the last." He went on to say, "Out of this may come something that will help all of them, and that is to be a better person, do a better job in playing basketball, or their studies or whatever it might be."

King Solomon warns us to be careful to "not boast about tomorrow, for you do not know what a day may bring forth." Even though none of us is promised a tomorrow here on earth, many people take life for granted. That is why Moses prayed in Psalm 90:12, "Teach us to number our days aright, that we may gain a heart of wisdom." Not only do we need to be prepared for death by trusting in Christ alone for forgiveness of sin and eternal life, but we also need to remember that each day is a precious gift. We each have the opportunity to either waste it or use it wisely to do something valuable and eternal.

An Unchanging God in Changing Times

There is a time for everything, and a season for every activity under heaven.   Ecclesiastes 3:1

He was benched by the Tampa Bay Buccaneers, told that he would not be their starting quarterback and eventually released. But one year later Trent Dilfer returned to Tampa to play in football's greatest game - the Super Bowl.

During the off-season he had been signed by the Baltimore Ravens to backup Tony Banks. But when Banks struggled early in the season Dilfer was given the starting nod. After losing his first game Dilfer then led the Ravens to 11 consecutive victories. Under his leadership the Ravens finished the season with a lop-sided win against the Giants in a Super Bowl that was played in the same city that cast him aside a year earlier.

Trent Dilfer is not only the winning quarterback from Super Bowl XXXV, he is also a Christian. He has known his share of disappointments and joys - and the last year certainly included both. After his triumphant return to Tampa, Dilfer stated, "The last month I've meditated on a verse in the Bible: Everything is possible for he who believes."

Life on earth promises us a variety of experiences: hardship and pleasure, sorrow and laughter, defeat and victory. The list goes on and on. Times are always changing, but our hope as Christians is to place our trust in an unchanging and almighty God who loves us with a perfect love. He will never leave us or forsake us, and knowing this we can rest in His strength and peace.

Whatever Circumstances May Come

For I have learned to be content whatever the circumstances. I know what it is to be in need, and I know what it is to have plenty. I have learned the secret of being content in any and every situation, whether well fed or hungry, whether living in plenty or in want. I can do everything through him who gives me strength.
Philippians 4:11-13

Derrick Mathis was a poverty-stricken 17-year-old whose mother was dying of lung cancer. While vacationing in Gulfport, Mississippi with friends during the summer before his senior year, Derrick saw the ocean for the first time. He had always wanted to go to the beach and enthusiastically sprinted across the sand and dove into the surf. But Derrick never got up. His head struck bottom, breaking his neck. When he was noticed floating face down Derrick was pulled to shore and given CPR by Good Samaritans. He was then rushed to the hospital and later flown back home to Memphis where doctors operated on his spine.

Even after the surgery Derrick was paralyzed below the waist, and though he could move his arms, he could not move his fingers. When he was moved into a rehabilitation hospital two months after the accident, Derrick became a cheerleader to the other patients and encouraged them to persevere. In the midst of his trials, which included losing his mother after a hard fought battle with cancer, Derrick still maintained hope. He said, "If you're down and out the situation is not going to get any better than it is already. You have to keep your high spirits, your high hopes and you will make it."

We certainly don't have the power to control all of the circumstances of life. But we do have the power to choose the attitude in which we respond to those circumstances. The Christian definition of contentment is an internal attitude of peace and satisfaction that is not dependent on outward circumstances.

Contagious Courage!

Now I want you to know, brothers, that what has happened to me has really served to advance the gospel. As a result, it has become clear thoughout the whole palace guard and to everyone else that I am in chains for Christ. Because of my chains, most of the brothers in the Lord have been encouraged to speak the word of God more courageously and fearlessly.   Philippians 1:12-14

During the 17th century George Fox and the Quakers were spreading the Gospel throughout England, and hundreds of people were being saved. While preaching at a revival meeting Fox was arrested and charged with blasphemy. Thrown into a filthy dungeon that was overrun with bugs, rats and the vilest of criminals, he was not allowed any visitors. When Christian friends tried to bring him food, they were chased away and clubbed by the guards.

Living nearly 150 miles from the prison was a 16-year-old crippled boy by the name of James Parnell. In spite of his handicap the teenager walked the entire distance to see George Fox. When he finally arrived the boy somehow managed to visit Fox. A Quaker historian states, "After he and George Fox spent some time in fellowship together, the lad left the Carlisle dungeon with heart aflame and gave the rest of his life to Christ."

Similarly, almost 2,000 years ago, the Apostle Paul was imprisoned because of his faith. In his letter to the Philippians he clearly states that because of his hardships, other Christians had been inspired to be bold and share the Good News of Jesus Christ. Time and time again history proves that courage is often contagious.

Someone Who Understands

For we do not have a high priest who is unable to sympathize with our weaknesses, but we have one who has been tempted in every way, just as we are--yet was without sin. Let us then approach the throne of grace with confidence, so that we may receive mercy and find grace to help us in our time of need. Hebrews 4:15-16

Jim Abbott was born without a right hand. But despite his apparent disability Jim attempted to play Little League baseball. He went on to play in high school and then became an All-American while playing college ball. Jim followed that up by helping the American team to a gold medal at the Olympics. He then became a pitcher in the Major Leagues and pitched his way to a no-hit, no-run game during the 1993 penant race.

Jim has a special place in his heart for disabled children and the challenges they face. On one occasion, he heard of a 5-year-old boy who had lost his hand in an accident and responded by writing the boy a very personal letter. In the letter he wrote of the big game in 1993 and said, " When the final out was made a lot of things went through my mind. The only thing I didn't pay attention to was my handicap. You see, it had nothing to do with anything."

Just as Jim has an understanding and sympathetic heart for boys and girls who face the challenges of being handicapped, Jesus, our high priest, is also understanding and sympathetic with us. Jesus humbled Himself and took on human flesh and bone. He dwelt among us and knows our trials and our temptations. Because of His great love, Jesus invites us to come to His throne of grace when we are in need and He will help us.

Some Things Are Worth Dying For

For you know that it was not with perishable things such as silver or gold that you were redeemed from the empty way of life handed down to you from your forefathers, but with the precious blood of Christ, a lamb without blemish or defect.   I Peter 1:18-19

Tension between the American colonies and Great Britain had been building for more than 10 years. Beginning in the 1760's the British has passed a number of laws that had increased their control over the 13 colonies. In an effort to decide what action to take against the British, representatives of the colonies met in 1775.

After listening to conservative members tell of their hope for peace with Great Britain, Patrick Henry stood to speak. In one of history's greatest speeches he boldy demanded, "Is life so dear, or peace so sweet, as to be purchased at the price of chains and slavery? Forbid it, Almighty God! I know what course others may take, but, as for me, give me liberty or give me death!" His powerful words were printed and distributed everywhere and helped convince the colonists to organize a militia and declare freedom from British rule.

The Revolutionary War began in 1775 in Lexington and ended eight years later with the surrender of the British at Yorktown. The war had proved costly for the Americans. Approximately 7,200 were killed in battle. Another 10,000 soldiers died in military camps because of disease or exposure to extreme weather conditions. In addition, nearly 8,500 captured Americans died in British prisons. Another 1,400 soldiers were missing. But the sacrifices by the American colonies resulted in freedom. In the place of British rule the colonies set up a government that guaranteed certain rights - including life, liberty and the pursuit of happiness.

The freedom that Christians have also came at a great price. Jesus paid for our freedom with His own innocent blood when He took our punishment and died on the cross. Through faith in Jesus and the price He paid, we are set free from the bondage of the law, the power of sin that once mastered our lives, and the punishment of sin and death. "It is for freedom that Christ has set us free" (Galatians 5:1).

Failure - And Then What?

Repent! Turn away from all your offenses; then sin will not be your downfall. Rid yourselves of all the offenses you have committed, and get a new heart and a new spirit.   Ezekiel 18:30-31

Thomas Edison was probably the world's greatest inventor. Though he had only three months of formal schooling, he patented over 1,100 inventions that literally changed the lives of billions of people. Such inventions included the electric light and the phonograph. Edison also came very close to inventing the radio, predicted the use of atomic energy and improved the inventions of others, such as the telephone, electric generator, typewriter, and motion picture.

Edison believed in the value of hard work and proved it by working for several days at a time while only stopping for brief naps. He once defined genius as "1% inspiration and 99% perspiration." Never discouraged by failure, he failed nearly 10,000 times while experimenting with the storage battery. Edison simply said, "Why, I have not failed. I've just found 10,000 ways that won't work."

We all fail - we all sin. The Bible tells us that "There is no one righteous, not even one" (Romans 3:10) and "all have sinned and fall short of the glory of God" (3:23). So - what should we do about it? The answer is simply this - **REPENT!**

The Bible instructs us over and over again to repent of our sin. But repentance is more than simply telling God that we're sorry. Someone once said that repentance is "being sorry enough about our sins to stop." On a similar note, II Corinthians 7:9-10 states that real sorrow leads to repentance. Therefore, repentance involves learning from our failures and then taking the appropriate steps to change.

The Power of Problems

And the God of all grace, who called you to his eternal glory in Christ, after you have suffered a little while, will himself restore you strong, firm and steadfast. To Him be the power for ever and ever. Amen.   I Peter 5:10-11

DID YOU KNOW?

• At 39, Franklin D. Roosevelt was crippled by polio and never again walked without braces or other aids. Yet, he became the only President to be elected to four terms of office.

• Before the age of two, an illness left Helen Keller blind, deaf and mute. Yet, she became a famous author and speaker and committed her life to helping others who were handicapped.

• Jim Abbott pitched the American baseball team to a gold medal in the Olympics even though he had been born without a right hand.

• John Milton wrote one of history's greatest poems, "Paradise Lost," after he had become blind.

• Winston Churchill overcame stuttering to become one of history's most powerful speakers. As Prime Minister, he inspired and led Great Britain to victory in World War II.

• Ray Charles and Stevie Wonder gained worldwide fame as pianists and singers though both were blind.

• When he was only 8 years old Glen Cunningham was terribly injured in a schoolhouse fire and almost lost both legs. Yet, later in life he was considered to be the "world's fastest human being" and won a gold medal in the Olympics.

• Beethoven wrote his finest music after he became deaf.

Benjamin Disraeli, the first Jewish Prime Minister of England, once stated, "There is no education like adversity." Adversities or problems have the power to test and prove the quality of our character. They also have the power to develop our character. Someone else once said, "The important thing about a problem is not its solution, but the strength we gain in finding the solution."

Self - LESS - ness

Make my joy complete by being like-minded, having the same love, being one in spirit and purpose. Do nothing out of selfish ambition or vain conceit, but in humility consider others better than yourselves. Each of you should look not only to your own interests, but also to the interests of others. Your attitude should be the same as that of Christ Jesus. Philippians 2:2-5

Mount Everest is the highest mountain in the world - rising 5 1/2 miles above sea level. Avalanches, crevasses, strong winds, and thin air have made climbing the steep mountain extremely dangerous. Many have tried to climb Everest since the British first saw it in the 1850's. But it was not until 1953 that Sir Edmund Hillary and his native guide,Tenzing Norgay, became the first men actually to reach the top.

On their way down the mountain, tragedy almost struck when Hillary lost his footing. But his trusted guide dug his ax into the ice, held tightly to the line, and saved Hillary from falling to his death. Some time later, when Tenzing Norgay was questioned about his heroic act, he humbly and simply said, "Mountain climbers always help each other."

"Christians always help each other." That statement should be true of all who follow Jesus Christ. His life is the very definition of one who lived unselfishly. Jesus Christ left the splendor of heaven, humbled Himself, and became a servant to man (Philippians 2:6-8). Just as He considered the interests and needs of others, so should we.

Confident Courage

Stand firm in the faith; be men of courage; be strong.

I Corinthians 16:13

Dr. Jonas Salk gained worldwide respect and won numerous awards for developing a vaccine that would prevent the disease Poliomyelitis. Polio, as it is commonly called, attacks the brain and spine, causing paralysis in 47 to 75 percent of the cases. In 1952, American doctors reported almost 58,000 cases of the disease, the highest number ever recorded.

Dr. Salk developed the vaccine amidst strong opposition by a number of doctors and researchers. It had literally taken him two years of painstaking and careful research, working sometimes 18 hours a day, seven days a week to arrive at his formula. Among the first humans to receive the trial vaccine were Salk, his wife, and three sons. Commenting later on his decision to test the vaccine on his own family, Dr. Salk explained, "I had the courage of my convictions."

Conviction is defined as a faith that is firmly established and confident. God's Word commands us to "stand firm in the faith, be men of courage, be strong." As Christians we are moved to great acts of courage when our faith and convictions are founded in the living God who created the universe and yet walks beside us as our Shepherd and Friend. Such faith and convictions provide us with strength, courage, and confidence to take on the challenges that lie before us.

Different But Unified

You are no longer foreigners and aliens, but fellow citizens with God's people and members of God's household, built on the foundation of the apostles and prophets, with Christ Jesus himself as the chief cornerstone. Ephesians 2:19-20

The blockbuster hit "Remember the Titans" is based on a remarkable true story that took place in Alexandria, Virginia when three high schools - two black and one white - were integrated in 1971. Tension grew as the former white coach was bypassed for the head football coaching position even though he had seniority and a history of winning. Instead, the position was given to black coach Herman Moore.

Against what seemed to be insurmountable odds both coaches found common ground and joined forces to shape a group of angry players - who were struggling with their prejudices - into a solid team that worked together to become a winning program. What the Titans were able to accomplish through mutual respect and cooperation helped unite the racially divided community in Alexandria, and the effects are still visible today.

By grace through faith, we are saved and brought into the family of God. Regardless of race or color, our foundation is the same Jesus Christ. And, while there is diversity in His Church (none of us is the same - we are all different), the distinguishing mark of the Church should be unity. To be healthy and to function according to God's plan, there must be unity among the family of God.

Looking Out For Others

Each one should use whatever gift he has received to serve others, faithfully administering God's grace in its various forms.

I Peter 4:10

A company of soldiers was laboring in vain to move an enormous timber. The corporal was standing at a distance shouting orders, but to no avail the log lay upon the ground unmoved. Along came a rider, who after having observed the struggle approached the corporal and simply asked, "Why don't you go and help the men?" Somewhat shocked and insulted by the question, the corporal answered, "Me? Sir, I am a corporal."

Dismounting his horse and joining the soldiers, the rider instructed the men to heave all at once. With his help the timber was moved easily. When the job was finished the rider quietly mounted his horse. But before leaving, he said to the corporal, "The next time you and your men find yourself faced with a job that seems too hard to handle send for me, the commander-in-chief." At this, the corporal finally realized who the stranger on horseback was who had been so willing to lend a hand. It was none other than George Washington.

The Bible teaches us in Philippians 2:3-4 "in humility consider others better than yourselves. Each of you should look not only to your own interests, but also to the interests of others." As we follow Jesus' example of servanthood, it is our responsibility to use the gifts, abilities, time and resources that God has given to each of us to help one another.

One Life to Live

For to me, to live is Christ and to die is gain.   Philippians 1:21

When Nathan Hale graduated from Yale College at the age of 18, he was among the top 13 highest ranking scholars. And though he intended to become a minister like his older brother, he began his professional career as a teacher in the public schools in Connecticut.

After American and British armies clashed at Lexington and Concord, Hale attended his town's meeting. And though he was not yet of age, he spoke to the entire gathering, "Let us march immediately and never lay down our arms until we obtain our independence." The next day Hale prayed with his students, said good-bye, and joined the army where he was commissioned as a lieutenant. His daring leadership in capturing a supply vessel under the guns of a British warship earned him a place in an elite fighting group called the "Rangers."

When the commander of the Rangers asked for a volunteer to sneak across enemy lines and bring back information on the position and plans of the British, the request was met with silence. Finally, the silence was broken when the Rangers' youngest captain, Nathan Hale, agreed to undertake the dangerous mission.

Disguised in civilian clothes, he made it across enemy lines and successfully gathered the much needed information. But as Hale returned on September 21, 1776, he was captured and sentenced to be executed as a spy. The British refused Hale's request for a Bible and marched him to an apple tree where he was hanged. In his dying speech, Nathan Hale spoke these words, "I only regret that I have but one life to lose for my country."

Paul stated his reason for living in his letter to the church at Philippi, "For to me, to live is Christ and to die is gain." When we understand as Paul did - who we are, why we are here, and where we are going - our lives take on a wonderful and powerful new meaning that helps us make it through even the most difficult days.

A Good Example

Don't let anyone look down on you because you are young, but set an example for the believers in speech, in life, in love, in faith, and in purity. I Timothy 4:12

As the nation's top quarterback, Danny Wuerffel of the Florida Gators refused to pose for *Playboy* magazine's All-American preseason team because of his commitment to follow Christ. He explained by making the statement, "That's not the type of person I would want to portray myself as."

Later that year during his senior season *Sports Illustrated* featured a story about Danny. The article told how reporters had snooped around trying to dig up some dirt on him only to find out that he did not curse, smoke, drink, chase girls, or cut class. What the reporters had discovered was that Danny carried a Bible to class, prayed twice a day, and held an NCAA passing record.

In December of 1996 when he received the Heisman Trophy as the nation's top college football player, Danny Wuerffel spoke to a nationally televised audience and said, "First and foremost, I want to give thanks to God. He is the rock upon which I stand." He went on to say, "The biggest blessing of all is having a living and loving relationship with Jesus."

The Christian life should be different. When others see us they should see Christ. But real Christian character is so much more than who we are in public. It also involves who we are in private. Someone once said that Christian character is "who we are when no one is looking." God desires that we consistently live what we believe - even when we think no one is looking.

Kindness Rewarded

Be kind and compassionate to one another.　　　Ephesians 4:32

Looking for a room to spend the night, an elderly couple entered a small hotel in Philadelphia. The man said to the young clerk, "All the other hotels are full. Can you give us a room?" The clerk responded, "There are three conventions that are simultaneously meeting in the city, and every hotel is full. There are no accommodations to be found anywhere." He then added, "Every one of our rooms is full, also. But I can't send a nice couple like you out into the rain at one o'clock in the morning. If you wouldn't mind, you could spend the night in my room."

Checking out the next morning the elderly man said to the clerk, "You know, you are the kind of manager that should be the boss of the finest hotel in the United States. Perhaps one day I will build one for you." The clerk simply laughed and soon forgot about the incident. He forgot until two years later when he unexpectedly received a letter from the couple inviting him to New York. Enclosed were two round trip tickets.

After arriving in New York the elderly gentleman took the clerk to the corner of Fifth Avenue and Thirty-fourth Street. He then directed his attention to a magnificent new building. The kindly old man stated, "This is the hotel that I have built for you to manage." That hotel was named the Waldorf-Astoria. The young clerk accepted the offer that day and became the manager of what was considered to be the finest hotel in all the world.

The New Testament word for "kindness" has a basic meaning of usefulness. The emphasis is on action. The Bible clearly communicates to us that the second greatest commandment is to "love your neighbor." But real love is useful and helpful. It is love in action and it is noticed by others, but more importantly, it is noticed by God.

What Are We Here For?

For we are God's workmanship, created in Christ Jesus to do good works, which God prepared in advance for us to do.

Ephesians 2:10

After an all night march through drenching rains and only two hours rest, the Union forces under General Hooker waged a fierce battle against the Confederates, who occupied Fort Magruder. Hooker's men fought bravely but were greatly outnumbered. By late afternoon, in the midst of heavy rains, Hooker's men had taken heavy losses, and their ammunition was nearly exhausted. Their lines were being driven back, and four of their big guns had fallen into the hands of the Confederates.

Seeing the guns fall into enemy hands was Michael Dillon, a Private in the Union army. Suddenly, the young private jumped to his feet, charged the enemy and begged for his comrades to join him in retaking the guns. His lieutenant yelled for Dillon to get down because he was drawing the enemy's fire. Private Dillon shouted back: "What are we here for?" He then rallied a group of boys like him and drove the Confederate army back. After being badly shot in the leg and having his gun blown from his hand by an exploding shell, Private Dillon picked up the gun of a fallen comrade and continued the fight until he finally saw the enemy repulsed.

What are we here for? That is an important question that needs an answer. For the Christian, the answer is found in Ephesians 2:10, "good works." God saves us from our sins and brings us into His family in order that we might do good works. According to Titus 2:14, because of our faith in Christ and our love for Christ, we should be "eager to do what is good."

Thanksgiving

Give thanks to Him and praise His name. For the LORD is good and His love endures forever; His faithfulness continues through all generations. Psalm 100:4-5

After studying medicine, Dr. David Livingstone traveled to South Africa to become a missionary. It didn't take long for him to notice that most mission stations were located along the coast. He dreamed of reaching people who had never heard the Good News of Jesus Christ, and he began to make plans to travel deep into Africa and establish a mission. After receiving permission to begin a new work 200 miles into the interior, he took an African teacher named Mebalwe and began construction of the mission station.

Approximately three months later he heard reports that lions were attacking cattle in a nearby village. Because the lions boldly attacked during the day and not at night, the local villagers believed they were devils and were afraid. Dr. Livingstone believed that if one of the lions were shot the others would scatter in fear. So he and Mebalwe left their work at the mission station and set out for the village.

Soon after their arrival a lion broke into one of the pens to attack the cattle. Dr. Livingstone fired his gun. As he reloaded, the lion sprang upon him and clamped down on his shoulder with its powerful jaws. Mebalwe tried to shoot the lion but his gun misfired. When it did the lion turned his attention to Mebalwe, and the beast sank his teeth into Mebalwe's leg. When another man tried to spear the lion it left Mebalwe and charged him. Suddenly, shots rang out and the lion dropped dead. The injured Dr. Livingstone had fired two bullets into the beast. Just as the doctor had said, the other lions scattered and never returned.

Both Dr. Livingstone and Mebalwe had been badly injured in the attack. Nevertheless, Dr. David Livingstone wrote his father in

Scotland, thankful that God had saved his life.

For the Christian, THANKSGIVING should be more than a holiday that comes once a year. The giving of thanks needs to become a daily discipline or practice as we learn to recognize God's goodness in our daily lives. According to God's Word, "Every good and perfect gift is from above, coming down from the Father of the heavenly lights" (James 1:18).